D0043173

GORDON JAMES BITNEY
405 - 675 W. HASTINGS ST.
VANCOUVER, B.C.   V6B 1N2
SOLICITOR
TEL. (604) 682-8504

HARRAP'S

French Grammar

Compiled by
LEXUS
with
Raymond Perrez,
Noël Peacock
and
Sabine Citron

HARRAP

EDINBURGH
PARIS   NEW YORK

Distributed in the United States by
PRENTICE HALL
New York

First published in Great Britain 1987
by HARRAP BOOKS Ltd
43–45 Annandale Street, Edinburgh EH7 4AZ
© *Harrap Limited* 1987

Reprinted 1988 (twice), 1990 (four times), 1991; 1992 (twice)

ISBN 0 245-54582-4

In the United States, ISBN 0-13-383316-X

Library of Congress Cataloging-in-Publication Data

Harrap's French grammar / compiled by Lexus with Raymond
    Perrex, Nöel Peacock, and Sabine Citron.
            p.   cm.
    ISBN 0-13-383316-X (soft) : $5.00
    1. French language – Grammar – 1950.
2. French language – Textbooks for foreign speakers – English.
I. Perrez, Raymond. II. Peacock, N.A. III. Citron, Sabine. IV.
    Lexus (Firm) V. Title: French grammar.
PC2112.H34 1990   89-70926
448.2′421 – dc20   CIP

Printed in England by Clays Ltd, St Ives plc

INTRODUCTION

This French grammar has been written to meet the new demands of language teaching in schools and colleges and is particularly suitable for exam revision. The essential rules of the French language have been set in terms that are as accessible as possible to all users. Where technical terms have been used then full explanations of these terms have also been supplied. There is also a full glossary of grammatical terminology on pages 9-14. While literary aspects of the French language have not been ignored, the emphasis has been placed squarely on modern spoken French. This grammar, with its wealth of lively and typical illustrations of usage taken from the present-day language, is the ideal study tool for all levels - from the beginner who is starting to come to grips with the French language through to the advanced user who requires a comprehensive and readily accessible work of reference.

Abbreviations used in the text:

fem   feminine
masc masculine
plur plural
sing singular

CONTENTS

1. GLOSSARY OF GRAMMATICAL TERMS

ADJECTIVE

A describing word, which adds information about a noun, telling us what something is like (eg *a small house*, *a red car*, *an interesting* pastime).

ADVERB

Adverbs are normally used with a verb to add extra information by indicating **how** the action is done (adverbs of manner), **when, where** and **with how much intensity** the action is done (adverbs of time, place and intensity), or **to what extent** the action is done (adverbs of quantity). Adverbs may also be used with an adjective or another adverb (eg *a very attractive girl*, *very well*).

AGREEMENT

In French, words such as adjectives, articles and pronouns are said to agree in number and gender with the noun or pronoun they refer to. This means that their spelling changes according to the **number** of the noun (singular or plural) and according to its **gender** (masculine or feminine).

ANTECEDENT

The antecedent of a relative pronoun is the word or words to which the relative pronoun refers. The antecedent is usually found directly before the relative pronoun (eg in the sentence *I know the man who did this*, *the man* is the antecedent of *who*).

APPOSITION

A word or a clause is said to be in apposition to another when it is placed directly after it without any joining word (eg *Mr Jones*, *our bank manager*, *rang today*).

ARTICLE	See DEFINITE ARTICLE, INDEFINITE ARTICLE and PARTITIVE ARTICLE.
AUXILIARY	The French auxiliary verbs, or 'helping' verbs, are **avoir** (*to have*) and **être** (*to be*). They are used to make up the first part of compound tenses, the second part being a past participle (eg *I have eaten*).
CARDINAL	Cardinal numbers are numbers such as *one*, *two*, *ten*, *fourteen*, as opposed to **ordinal** numbers (eg *first*, *second*).
CLAUSE	A clause is a group of words which contains at least a subject and a verb: *he said* is a clause. A clause often contains more than this basic information, eg *he said this to her yesterday*. Sentences can be made up of several clauses, eg *he said/he'd call me /if he were free*. See SENTENCE.
COMPARATIVE	The comparative forms of adjectives and adverbs allow us to compare two things, persons or actions. In English, *more … than*, *…er than*, *less … than* and *as … as* are used for comparison.
COMPOUND	Compound tenses are verb tenses consisting of more than one element. In French, the compound tenses of a verb are formed by the **auxiliary** verb and the **past participle**: *j'ai visité*, *il est venu*.
CONDITIONAL	This mood is used to describe what someone would do, or something that would happen if a condition were fulfilled (eg *I would come if I were well*; *the chair would have broken if he had sat on it*).
CONJUGATION	The conjugation of a verb is the set of different forms taken in the particular tenses of that verb.
CONJUNCTION	Conjunctions are linking words. They may be coordinating or subordinating. Coordinating conjunctions are words like *and*, *but*, *or*; subordinating conjunctions are words like *because*, *after*, *although*.

DEFINITE ARTICLE The definite article is *the* in English and *le, la* and *les* in French.

DEMONSTRATIVE Demonstrative adjectives (eg *this, that, these*) and pronouns (eg *this one, that one*) are used to point out a particular person or object.

DIRECT OBJECT A noun or a pronoun which in English follows a verb without any linking preposition, eg *I met a friend*.

ELISION Elision consists in replacing the last letter of certain words (*le, la, je, me, te, se, de, que*) with an apostrophe (') before a word starting with a **vowel** or a **silent h** (eg *l'eau, l'homme, j'aime*).

ENDING The ending of a verb is determined by the **person** (1st/2nd/3rd) and **number** (singular/plural) of its subject. In French, most tenses have six different endings. See PERSON and NUMBER.

EXCLAMATION Words or sentences used to express surprise, wonder (eg *what!, how!, how lucky!, what a nice day!*).

FEMININE See GENDER.

GENDER The gender of a noun indicates whether the noun is **masculine** or **feminine** (all French nouns are either masculine or feminine).

IDIOMATIC Idiomatic expressions (or idioms), are expressions which cannot normally be translated word for word. For example, *it's raining cats and dogs* is translated by *il pleut des cordes*.

IMPERATIVE A mood used for giving orders (eg *eat!, don't go!*).

INDEFINITE Indefinite pronouns and adjectives are words that do not refer to a definite person or object (eg *each, someone, every*).

INDEFINITE ARTICLE The indefinite article is *a* in English and *un, une* and *des* in French.

INDICATIVE The normal form of a verb as in *I like, he came, we are trying*. It is opposed to the subjunctive, conditional and imperative.

INDIRECT OBJECT	A pronoun or noun which follows a verb indirectly, with a linking preposition (usually **to**), eg *I spoke to my friend/him.*
INFINITIVE	The infinitive is the basic form of the verb as found in dictionaries. Thus *to eat, to finish, to take* are infinitives. In French, the infinitive is recognized by its ending: *manger, finir, prendre.*
INTERROGATIVE	Interrogative words are used to ask a question. This may be a direct question (*when will you arrive?*) or an indirect question (*I don't know when he'll arrive*). See QUESTION.
MASCULINE	See GENDER.
MOOD	The name given to the four main areas within which a verb is conjugated. See INDICATIVE, SUBJUNCTIVE, CONDITIONAL, IMPERATIVE.
NOUN	A naming word, which can refer to living creatures, things, places or abstract ideas, eg *postman, cat, shop, passport, life.*
NUMBER	The number of a noun indicates whether the noun is **singular** or **plural**. A singular noun refers to one single thing or person (eg *boy, train*) and a plural noun to several (eg *boys, trains*).
ORDINAL	Ordinal numbers are *first, second, third, fourth* and all other numbers which end in **-th**. In French, all ordinal numbers, except for *premier* (first) and *second* (second), end in **-ième**.
PARTITIVE ARTICLE	The partitive articles are *some* and *any* in English and *du, de la* and *des* (as in *du pain, de la confiture, des bananes*) in French.
PASSIVE	A verb is used in the passive when the subject of the verb does not perform the action but is subjected to it. The passive is formed with the verb **to be** and the past participle of the verb, eg *he was rewarded.*

PAST PARTICIPLE	The past participle of a verb is the form which is used after **to have** in English, eg *I have eaten*, *I have said*, *you have tried*.
PERSON	In any tense, there are three persons in the singular (1st: *I* ..., 2nd: *you* ..., 3rd: *he/she* ...), and three in the plural (1st: *we* ..., 2nd: *you* ..., 3rd: *they* ...). See also ENDING.
PERSONAL PRONOUNS	Personal pronouns stand for a noun. They usually accompany a verb and can be either the subject (*I, you, he/she/it, we, they*) or the object of the verb (*me, you, him/her/it, us, them*).
PLURAL	See NUMBER.
POSSESSIVE	Possessive adjectives and pronouns are used to indicate possession or ownership. They are words like *my/mine, your/yours, our/ours*.
PREPOSITION	Prepositions are words such as *with, in, to, at*. They are followed by a noun or a pronoun.
PRESENT PARTICIPLE	The present participle is the verb form which ends in **-ing** in English (**-ant** in French).
PRONOUN	A word which stands for a noun. The main categories of pronouns are: ★ **Relative pronouns** (eg *who, which, that*) ★ **Interrogative pronouns** (eg *who?, what?, which?*) ★ **Demonstrative pronouns** (eg *this, that, these*) ★ **Possessive pronouns** (eg *mine, yours, his*) ★ **Personal pronouns** (eg *you, him, us*) ★ **Reflexive pronouns** (eg *myself, himself*) ★ **Indefinite pronouns** (eg *something, all*)
QUESTION	There are two question forms: **direct** questions stand on their own and require a question mark at the end (eg *when will he come?*); **indirect** questions are introduced by a clause and require no question mark (eg *I wonder when he will come*).

REFLEXIVE	Reflexive verbs 'reflect' the action back onto the subject (eg *I dressed myself*). They are always found with a reflexive pronoun and are much more common in French than in English.
SENTENCE	A sentence is a group of words made up of one or more clauses (see CLAUSE). The end of a sentence is indicated by a punctuation mark (usually a full stop, a question mark or an exclamation mark).
SILENT H	The name 'silent **h**' is actually misleading since an **h** is never pronounced in French. The point is that, when a silent **h** occurs, any preceding vowel is not pronounced either. For example, the **h** in *j'habite* is silent (note the *j'*). The **h** in *je hurle* is not silent (note the **je**).
SIMPLE TENSE	Simple tenses are tenses in which the verb consists of one word only, eg *j'habite*, *Maurice partira*.
SINGULAR	See NUMBER.
SUBJECT	The subject of a verb is the noun or pronoun which performs the action. In the sentences *the train left early* and *she bought a record*, *the train* and *she* are the subjects.
SUBJUNCTIVE	The subjunctive is a verb form which is rarely used in English (eg *if I were you*, *God save the Queen*), but common in French.
SUPERLATIVE	The form of an adjective or an adverb which, in English, is marked by *the most ...*, *the ...est* or *the least ...*.
TENSE	Verbs are used in tenses, which tell us when an action takes place, eg in the present, the imperfect, the future.
VERB	A 'doing' word, which usually describes an action (eg *to sing*, *to work*, *to watch*). Some verbs describe a state (eg *to be*, *to have*, *to hope*).

2. ARTICLES

A. THE DEFINITE ARTICLE

1. Forms

In English, there is only one form of the definite article: **the.** In French, there are three forms, depending on the gender and number of the noun following the article:

— with a masculine singular noun: **le**
— with a feminine singular noun: **la** } the
— with a plural noun (masc or fem): **les**

MASC SING	FEM SING	PLURAL
le chauffeur the driver	**la secrétaire** the secretary	**les étudiants** the students
le salon the lounge	**la cuisine** the kitchen	**les chambres** the bedrooms

Note: **le** and **la** both change to **l'** before a vowel or a silent **h**:

	MASCULINE	FEMININE
BEFORE VOWEL	**l'avion** the plane	**l'odeur** the smell
BEFORE SILENT H	**l'homme** the man	**l'hôtesse** the hostess

Pronunciation: the **s** of **les** is pronounced **z** when the noun following it begins with a vowel or a silent **h**.

2. Forms with the prepositions 'à' and 'de'

When the definite article is used with **à** or **de**, the following spelling changes take place:

a) *with à (to, at)*

à + le	→	au
à + les	→	aux

à + la and à + l' do not change

au restaurant	**aux enfants**
at/to the restaurant	to the children
à la plage	**à l'aéroport**
at/to the beach	at/to the airport

Pronunciation: the **x** of **aux** is pronounced **z** when the noun following it begins with a vowel or a silent **h.**

b) *with* **de** *(of, from)*

de + le	→	du
de + les	→	des

de + **la** and **de** + **l'** do not change

du directeur	**des chômeurs**
of/from the manager	of/from the unemployed
de la région	**de l'usine**
of/from the area	of/from the factory

Pronunciation: the **s** of **des** is pronounced **z** when the noun following it begins with a vowel or a silent **h.**

3. Use

As in English, the definite article is used when referring to a particular person or thing, or particular persons or things:

les amis dont je t'ai parlé	**le café est prêt**
the friends I told you about	the coffee is ready

However, the definite article is used far more frequently in French than in English. It is used in particular in the following cases where English uses no article:

a) *when the noun is used in a general sense*

i) to refer to all things of a kind:

vous acceptez les chèques ?
do you accept cheques?

le sucre est mauvais pour les dents
sugar is bad for the teeth

ii) to refer to abstract things:

le travail et les loisirs	**la musique classique**
work and leisure	classical music

iii) when stating likes and dislikes:

j'aime la viande, mais je préfère le poisson
I like meat, but I prefer fish

je déteste les tomates
I hate tomatoes

b) *with geographical names*

i) continents, countries and areas:

le Canada Canada	**la France** France	**l'Europe** Europe
la Bretagne Brittany	**l'Afrique** Africa	**les Etats-Unis** the United States

But: the article **la** is omitted with the prepositions **en** (to, in) and **de** (from):

j'habite en France   **il vient d'Italie**
I live in France   he comes from Italy

ii) mountains, lakes and rivers:

le mont Everest   **le lac de Genève**
Mount Everest   Lake Geneva

c) *with names of seasons*

l'automne	autumn
l'hiver	winter
le printemps	spring
l'été	summer

But: **en automne/été/hiver**
in autumn/summer/winter

au printemps   **un jour d'été**
in spring   a summer's day

d) *with names of languages*

j'apprends le français
I'm learning French

But: **ce film est en anglais**
this film is in English

e) *with parts of the body*

    j'ai les cheveux roux   **ouvrez la bouche**
    I've got red hair   open your mouth

    les mains en l'air !   **l'homme à la barbe noire**
    hands up!   the man with the black beard

f) *with names following an adjective*

    le petit Pierre   **la pauvre Isabelle**
    little Pierre   poor Isabelle

g) *with titles*

    le docteur Coste   **le commandant Cousteau**
    Doctor Coste   Captain Cousteau

h) *with days of the week to express regular occurrences*

    que fais-tu le samedi ?
    what do you do on Saturdays?

i) *with names of subjects or leisure activities*

    les maths   **l'histoire et la géographie**
    maths   history and geography

    la natation, la lecture, le football
    swimming, reading, football

j) *in expressions of price, quantity etc*

    c'est combien le kilo/la douzaine/la bouteille ?
    how much is it for a kilo/dozen/bottle?

B. THE INDEFINITE ARTICLE

1. Forms

In French, there are three forms of the indefinite article, depending on the number and gender of the noun it accompanies:

— with a masculine singular noun: **un**   a
— with a feminine singular noun: **une**   a
— with a plural noun (masc or fem): **des**   some

Note: **des** is often not translated in English:

> **il y a des nuages dans le ciel**
> there are clouds in the sky

2. Use

a) On the whole, the French indefinite article is used in the same way as its English equivalent:

un homme	**une femme**	**des hommes/ femmes**
a man	a woman	(some) men/ women
un livre	**une tasse**	**des livres/tasses**
a book	a cup	(some) books/cups

b) However, the English indefinite article is not always translated in French:

i) when stating someone's profession or occupation:

> **mon père est architecte**
> my father is an architect

> **elle est médecin**
> she is a doctor

But: the article is used after **c'est**, **c'était** etc:

> **c'est un acteur célèbre**
> he's a famous actor

> **ce sont des fraises**
> these are strawberries

ii) with nouns in apposition:

Madame Leclerc, employée de bureau
Mrs Leclerc, an office worker

iii) after **quel** in exclamations:

quel dommage !   **quelle surprise !**
what a pity!   what a surprise!

c) In negative sentences, **de** (or **d'**) is used instead of **un, une, des**:

je n'ai pas d'amis   **je n'ai plus de voiture**
I don't have any friends   I don't have a car any more

d) In French (but not in English), the indefinite article is used with abstract nouns followed by an adjective:

avec une patience remarquable
with remarkable patience

elle a fait des progrès étonnants
she's made amazing progress

But: the article is not used when there is no adjective:

avec plaisir   **sans hésitation**
with pleasure   without hesitation

C. THE PARTITIVE ARTICLE

1. Forms

There are three forms of the French partitive article, which corresponds to 'some'/'any' in English:

— with a masculine singular noun: **du**
— with a feminine singular noun: **de la**
— with plural nouns (masc or fem): **des**

du vin	**de la bière**	**des fruits**
some wine	some beer	some fruit

Note: **de l'** is used in front of masculine or feminine singular nouns beginning with a vowel or a silent **h**:

de l'argent   **de l'eau**
some money   some water

2. Use

a) On the whole, the French partitive article is used as in English. However, English tends to omit the partitive article where French does not:

achète du pain   **vous avez du beurre ?**
buy (some) bread   do you have (any) butter?

je voudrais de la viande   **tu veux de la soupe ?**
I'd like some meat   do you want (any) soup?

tu dois manger des légumes
you must eat (some) vegetables

as-tu acheté des poires ?
did you buy any pears?

b) The partitive article is replaced by **de** (or **d'**) in the following cases:

i) in negative expressions:

il n'y a plus de café   **je n'ai pas de verres**
there isn't any coffee left   I don't have any glasses

But: **ce n'est pas du cuir, c'est du plastique**
it's not leather, it's plastic

je n'ai que de l'argent français
I have only French money

ii) after expressions of quantity (see also p 219-20):

il boit trop de café   **il gagne assez d'argent**
he drinks too much coffee   he earns enough money

iii) after **avoir besoin de**:

j'ai besoin d'argent   **tu as besoin de timbres ?**
I need (some) money   do you need (any) stamps?

iv) where an adjective is followed by a plural noun:

de grands enfants   **de petites villes**
(some) tall children   (some) small towns

But: if the adjective comes after the noun, **des** does not change:

des résultats encourageants
encouraging results

3. Partitive or definite article?

When no article is used in English, be careful to use the right article in French: **le/la/les** or **du/de la/des**?

If **some/any** can be inserted before the English noun, the French partitive article should be used. But if the noun is used in a general sense and inserting **some/any** in front of the English noun does not make sense, the definite article must be used:

did you buy fish? (*ie any fish*)
tu as acheté *du* poisson ?

yes, I did; I like fish (*ie fish in general*)
oui ; j'aime *le* poisson

3. NOUNS

Nouns are naming words, which refer to persons, animals, things, places or abstract ideas.

A. GENDER

All French nouns are either masculine or feminine; there is no neuter as in English. Though no absolute rule can be stated, the gender can often be determined either by the meaning or the ending of the noun.

1. Masculine

a) *by meaning*

i) names of people and animals:

un homme	**le boucher**	**le tigre**
a man	the butcher	the tiger

ii) names of common trees and shrubs:

le chêne	**le sapin**	**le laurier**
the oak	the fir tree	the laurel

But:

une aubépine	**la bruyère**
a hawthorn	the heather

iii) days, months, seasons:

lundi	**mars**	**le printemps**
Monday	March	spring

iv) languages:

le français	**le polonais**	**le russe**
French	Polish	Russian

v) rivers and countries not ending in a silent e:

le Nil	**le Portugal**	**le Danemark**
the Nile	Portugal	Denmark

But:

le Danube	**le Rhône**	**le Mexique**
the Danube	the Rhone	Mexico

b) *by ending*

-acle	**le spectacle** (show)
	But: **une débâcle** (shambles)
-age	**le fromage** (cheese)
	But: **la cage** (cage), **une image** (picture), **la nage** (swimming), **la page** (page), **la plage** (beach), **la rage** (rage, rabies)
-é	**le marché** (market)
	But: nouns ending in **-té** and **-tié** (see p 26)
-eau	**le chapeau** (hat)
	But: **l'eau** (water), **la peau** (skin)
-ège	**le piège** (trap), **le collège** (secondary school)
-ème	**le thème** (theme, topic)
	But: **la crème** (the cream)
-isme, -asme	**le communisme** (communism), **le tourisme** (tourism), **l'enthousiasme** (enthusiasm)
-o	**le numéro** (the number)
	But: **la dynamo** (dynamo) and most abbreviated expressions: **une auto** (car), **la météo** (weather forecast), **la photo** (photograph), **la radio** (radio), **la sténo** (shorthand), **la stéréo** (stereo)

Nouns ending in a *consonant* are usually *masculine*.

Notable exceptions are:

i)   most nouns ending in **-tion**, **-sion**, **-ation**, **-aison**, **-ison**

ii) most abstract nouns ending in **-eur** (see p 26)

iii) the following nouns ending in a consonant:

la clef (key)	**la nef** (nave)
la soif (thirst)	**la faim** (hunger)
la fin (end)	**la façon** (manner)
la leçon (lesson)	**la boisson** (drink)
la moisson (harvest)	**la rançon** (ransom)
la mer (sea)	**la cuiller** (spoon)
la chair (flesh)	**la basse-cour** (farmyard)
la cour (yard)	**la tour** (tower)

la brebis (ewe)	**une fois** (once)
la vis (screw)	**la souris** (mouse)
la part (share)	**la plupart** (majority, most)
la dent (tooth)	**la dot** (dowry)
la forêt (forest)	**la jument** (mare)
la mort (death)	**la nuit** (night)
la croix (cross)	**la noix** (nut)
la paix (peace)	**la perdrix** (partridge)
la toux (cough)	**la voix** (voice)

2. Feminine

a) *by meaning*

i) names of females (people and animals):

la mère	**la bonne**	**la génisse**
the mother	the maid	the heifer

ii) names of rivers and countries ending in a silent e:

la Seine	**la Russie**	**la Belgique**
the Seine	Russia	Belgium

iii) saints days and festivals:

la Toussaint	**la Pentecôte**
All Saints' Day	Whitsun

But: **Noël** (Christmas) is masculine except with the definite article: **à la Noël** (at Christmas)

b) *by ending*

-ace	**la place** (square, seat)
	But: **un espace** (space)
-ade	**la salade** (salad)
	But: **le grade** (degree, rank), **le stade** (stadium)
-ance, -anse	**la puissance** (power), **la danse** (dancing)
-ée	**la soirée** (evening)
	But: **le musée** (museum), **le lycée** (secondary school)
-ence, -ense	**une évidence** (evidence), **la défense** (defence)
	But: **le silence** (silence)

-ère	la **lumière** (light) *But:* le **mystère** (mystery), le **caractère** (character)
-eur	la **peur** (fear) *But:* le **bonheur** (happiness), le **chœur** (choir), le **cœur** (heart), un **honneur** (honour), le **labeur** (toil), le **malheur** (misfortune)
-ie	la **pluie** (rain) *But:* le **génie** (genius), un **incendie** (fire), le **parapluie** (umbrella)
-ière	la **bière** (beer) *But:* le **cimetière** (cemetery)
-oire	la **gloire** (glory) *But:* le **laboratoire** (laboratory), le **pourboire** (tip)
-tion, -sion, -ation, -aison, -ison	la **fiction** (fiction), la **nation** (nation), la **raison** (reason), la **prison** (prison)
-té	la **bonté** (goodness) *But:* le **côté** (side), le **comté** (county), le **traité** (treaty), le **pâté** (pâté)
-tié	la **moitié** (half), la **pitié** (pity)

Most nouns ending in a silent e following two consonants:

la **botte** (boot), la **couronne** (crown), la **terre** (earth), la **masse** (mass), la **lutte** (struggle)

But: le **verre** (glass), le **parterre** (flower-bed), le **tonnerre** (thunder), un **intervalle** (interval), le **carosse** (carriage)

3. Difficulties

a) some nouns may have either gender depending on the sex of the person to whom they refer:

un artiste	**une artise**
a (male) artist	a (female) artist
le Russe	**la Russe**
the Russian (man)	the Russian (woman)

similarly:

un aide/une aide	an assistant
un camarade/une camarade	a friend
un domestique/une domestique	a servant
un enfant/une enfant	a child
un malade/une malade	a patient
un propriétaire/une propriétaire	an owner

b) others have only one gender for both sexes:

un ange	**un amateur**	**un auteur**
an angel	an amateur	an author(ess)
une connaissance	**la dupe**	**un écrivain**
an acquaintance	the dupe	a writer
Sa Majesté	**le médecin**	**le peintre**
His/Her Majesty	the doctor	the painter
une personne	**le poète**	**le professeur**
a person	the poet(ess)	the teacher
la recrue	**le sculpteur**	**la sentinelle**
the recruit	the sculptor (sculptress)	the sentry
le témoin	**la victime**	**la vedette**
the witness	the victim	the (film) star

c) the following nouns change meaning according to gender:

	MASCULINE	FEMININE
aide	male assistant	assistance, female assistant
crêpe	mourning band	pancake
critique	critic	criticism
faux	forgery	scythe

	MASCULINE	FEMININE
livre	book	pound
manche	handle	sleeve
manoeuvre	labourer	manoeuvre
mémoire	memorandum	memory
mode	method, way	fashion
mort	dead man	death
moule	mould	mussel
page	pageboy	page
pendule	pendulum	clock
physique	physique	physics
poêle	stove	frying pan
poste	post (*job*), set	post office
somme	nap	sum
tour	trick, tour	tower
trompette	trumpeter	trumpet
vapeur	steamer	steam
vase	vase	silt
voile	veil	sail

d) **gens** is regarded as feminine when it follows an adjective, and masculine when it precedes it:

de bonnes gens	**des gens ennuyeux**
good people	bores

B.   THE FORMATION OF FEMININES

The feminine of nouns may be formed in the following ways:

1. Add an 'e' to the masculine

un ami	**une amie**
a (male) friend	a (female) friend
un Hollandais	**une Hollandaise**
a Dutchman	a Dutch woman

a) nouns which end in **e** in the masculine do not change:

un élève	**une élève**
a (male) pupil	a (female) pupil

b) the addition of **e** often entails an alteration of the masculine form:

i) nouns ending in **t** and **n** double the final consonant:

le chien	**la chienne** (dog/bitch)
le chat	**la chatte** (cat)

ii) nouns ending in **-er** add a grave accent to the **e** before the silent **e**:

un ouvrier	**une ouvrière** (workman/female worker)

iii) nouns ending in **-eur** change into **-euse**:

le vendeur	**la vendeuse** (male/female shop assistant)

a few nouns ending in **-eur** change into **-eresse**:

le pécheur	**la pécheresse** (sinner)

iv) nouns ending in **-teur** change into **-teuse** or **-trice** according to the following guidelines:

if the stem of the word is also that of a present participle the feminine form is in **-euse**:

le chanteur	**la chanteuse** (male/female singer)

but if the stem is not that of a present participle, the feminine form is in **-trice**:

le lecteur	**la lectrice** (male/female reader)

v) nouns ending in **f** change to **-ve**:

le veuf	**la veuve** (widower/widow)

vi) nouns ending in **x** change to **-se**:

un époux   **une épouse** (husband/wife)

vii) nouns ending in **-eau** change to **-elle** :

le jumeau   **la jumelle** (male/female twin)

2. Use a different word (as in English)

le beau-fils	la belle-fille (son/daughter-in-law)
le beau-père	la belle-mère (father/mother-in-law)
le bélier	la brebis (ram/ewe)
le bœuf	la vache (ox/cow)
le canard	la cane (drake/duck)
le cheval	la jument (horse/mare)
le cerf	la biche (stag/hind)
le coq	la poule (cock/hen)
le fils	la fille (son/daughter)
le frère	la sœur (brother/sister)
un homme	une femme (man/woman)
un jars	une oie (gander/goose)
le mâle	la femelle (male/female)
le neveu	la nièce (nephew/niece)
un oncle	une tante (uncle/aunt)
le parrain	la marraine (godfather/godmother)
le père	la mère (father/mother)
le porc	la truie (pig/sow)
le roi	la reine (king/queen)

3. Add the word **femme** (or **femelle** for animals)

une femme poète (poetess)
un perroquet femelle (female parrot)

4. Irregular feminines

un abbé	une abbesse (abbot/abbess)
un âne	une ânesse (donkey)
le comte	la comtesse (count/countess)
le dieu	la déesse (god/goddess)
le duc	la duchesse (duke/duchess)
un Esquimau	une Esquimaude (Eskimo)
le fou	la folle (madman/mad woman)
un héros	une héroïne (hero/heroine)
un hôte	une hôtesse (host/hostess)
le maître	la maîtresse (master/mistress)
le prêtre	la prêtresse (priest/priestess)
le prince	la princesse (prince/princess)
le tigre	la tigresse (tiger/tigress)
le Turc	la Turque (Turk)
le vieux	la vieille (old man/old woman)

C.   THE FORMATION OF PLURALS

1. Most nouns form their plural by adding s to the singular: :

| le vin | les vins | wine |
| un étudiant | des étudiants | student |

2. Nouns ending in 's', '**x**' or '**z**' remain unchanged:

le bras	les bras	arm
la voix	les voix	voice
le nez	les nez	nose

3. Nouns ending in -**au**, -**eau** and -**eu** add x to the singular:

le tuyau	les tuyaux	drain-pipe
le bateau	les bateaux	boat
le jeu	les jeux	game

But:

le landau	les landaus	pram
le bleu	les bleus	bruise
le pneu	les pneus	tyre

4. Nouns ending in -**al** change to -**aux**:

| le journal | les journaux | newspaper |

But:

le bal	les bals	dance
le carnaval	les carnavals	carnival
le festival	les festivals	festival

5. Nouns ending in -**ail** change to -**aux**:

le bail	les baux	lease
le travail	les travaux	work
le vitrail	les vitraux	stained-glass window

Common exceptions in which the plural is formed in -**ail**:

le chandail	les chandails	sweater
le détail	les détails	detail
l'épouvantail	les épouvantails	scarecrow
l'éventail	les éventails	fan
le rail	les rails	rail

6. Nouns ending in *-ou*:

a) seven nouns ending in **-ou** add **x** in the plural:

le bijou	les bijoux	jewel
le caillou	les cailloux	pebble
le chou	les choux	cabbage
le genou	les genoux	knee
le hibou	les hiboux	owl
le joujou	les joujoux	toy
le pou	les poux	louse

b) other nouns ending in **-ou** add **s**:

le clou	les clous	nail

7. Plural of compound nouns

Each noun ought to be checked individually in a dictionary:

eg	le chou-fleur	les choux-fleurs	cauliflower
	le beau-père	les beaux-pères	father-in-law
But:	un essuie-glace	des essuie-glaces	windscreen wiper
	le tire-bouchon	les tire-bouchons	corkscrew

8. Irregular plurals:

un œil	des yeux	eye
le ciel	les cieux	sky
Monsieur	Messieurs	Mr
Madame	Mesdames	Mrs
Mademoiselle	Mesdemoiselles	Miss

9. Collective nouns

a) *singular in French but plural in English*

le bétail	cattle
la famille	family
la police	police

la police *a* arrêté certains grévistes
the police *have* arrested some strikers

b) *plural in French but singular in English*

les nouvelles sont bonnes
the news is good

10. Proper nouns

a) Ordinary family names are invariable:

> **j'ai rencontré les Leblanc**
> I met the Leblancs

b) Historical names add **-s**:

les Stuarts	**les Bourbons**	**les Tudors**
the Stuarts	the Bourbons	the Tudors

4. ADJECTIVES

Adjectives are describing words which usually accompany a noun (or a pronoun) and tell us what someone or something is like:

une *grande* ville	un passe-temps *intéressant*
a *large* city	an *interesting* pastime
elle est *espagnole*	c'était *ennuyeux*
she is *Spanish*	it was *boring*

A. AGREEMENT OF ADJECTIVES

In French, adjectives agree in number and gender with the noun or pronoun they refer to. This means that, unlike English adjectives, which don't change, French adjectives have four different forms which are determined by the noun they go with:

— **masculine singular** for masculine singular words (basic form, found in the dictionary)
— **feminine singular** for feminine singular words
— **masculine plural** for masculine plural words
— **feminine plural** for feminine plural words

un passeport *vert*	une voiture *verte*
a green passport	a green car
des gants *verts*	des chaussettes *vertes*
green gloves	green socks

Note: If two singular words share the same adjective, the adjective will be in the plural:

un foulard et un bonnet *rouges*
a red scarf and (a red) hat

If one of these words is feminine, one masculine, the adjective will be masculine plural:

une robe et un manteau *noirs*
a black dress and (a black) coat

B. FEMININE FORMS OF ADJECTIVES

1. General rule

Add the letter **e** to the masculine singular form:

MASCULINE	FEMININE
grand	**grande**
amusant	**amusante**
anglais	**anglaise**
bronzé	**bronzée**
un livre amusant an amusing book	**une histoire amusante** an amusing story
il est bronzé he is suntanned	**elle est bronzée** she is suntanned

2. Adjectives already ending in 'e'

These do not change:

MASCULINE	FEMININE
rouge	**rouge**
jeune	**jeune**
malade	**malade**
mon père est malade my father is ill	**ma mère est malade** my mother is ill

3. Others

The spelling of some adjectives changes when the **e** is added:

a) The following masculine endings generally double the final consonant before adding **e**:

MASCULINE ENDING	FEMININE ENDING
-el	**-elle**
-eil	**-eille**
-en	**-enne**
-on	**-onne**
-as	**-asse**
-et	**-ette**

MASCULINE		FEMININE
réel	(real)	réelle
cruel	(cruel)	cruelle
pareil	(similar)	pareille
ancien	(old)	ancienne
italien	(Italian)	italienne
bon	(good)	bonne
gras	(greasy)	grasse
bas	(low)	basse
muet	(dumb)	muette
net	(clear)	nette

un problème actuel   **la vie actuelle**
a topical problem   present-day life

un bon conseil   **c'est une bonne recette**
good advice   it's a good recipe

But: the feminine ending of some common adjectives in **-et** is **-ète** instead of **-ette**:

MASCULINE		FEMININE
complet	(complete)	complète
incomplet	(incomplete)	incomplète
concret	(concrete)	concrète
discret	(discreet)	discrète
inquiet	(worried)	inquiète
secret	(secret)	secrète

b) MASCULINE   FEMININE
    IN **-er**   IN **-ère**

cher	(dear)	chère
fier	(proud)	fière
dernier	(last)	dernière

c) MASCULINE   FEMININE
    IN **-x**   IN **-se**

heureux	(happy)	heureuse
malheureux	(unhappy)	malheureuse
sérieux	(serious)	sérieuse
jaloux	(jealous)	jalouse

But:	**doux**	(soft)	**douce**
	faux	(false)	**fausse**
	roux	(red-haired)	**rousse**
	vieux	(old)	**vieille**

d)

MASCULINE IN **-eur**		FEMININE IN **-euse**
menteur	(lying)	**menteuse**
trompeur	(deceitful)	**trompeuse**

But: This rule applies only when the stem of the adjective is also the stem of a present participle (eg **mentant**, **trompant**). The following five adjectives simply add an **e** to the feminine, **-eur** becoming **-eure**:

MASCULINE		FEMININE
extérieur	(external)	**extérieure**
intérieur	(internal)	**intérieure**
inférieur	(inferior)	**inférieure**
supérieur	(superior)	**supérieure**
meilleur	(better)	**meilleure**

The feminine ending of the remaining adjectives in **-teur** is **-trice**:

MASCULINE		FEMININE
protecteur	(protective)	**protectrice**
destructeur	(destructive)	**destructrice**

e)

MASCULINE IN **-f**		FEMININE IN **-ve**
neuf	(new)	**neuve**
vif	(lively)	**vive**
naïf	(naive)	**naïve**
actif	(active)	**active**
passif	(passive)	**passive**
positif	(positive)	**positive**
bref	(brief)	**brève** (note the **è**!)

f)

MASCULINE IN **-c**		FEMININE IN **-che** or **-que**
blanc	(white)	**blanche**
franc	(frank)	**franche**
sec	(dry)	**sèche** (note the **è**!)
public	(public)	**publique**
turc	(Turkish)	**turque**
grec	(Greek)	**grecque** (note the **c**!)

g) The following five common adjectives have an irregular feminine form and two forms for the masculine singular; the second masculine form, based on the feminine form, is used before words starting with a vowel or a silent **h**:

MASCULINE	FEMININE	MASCULINE 2
beau (beautiful)	**belle**	**bel**
nouveau (new)	**nouvelle**	**nouvel**
vieux (old)	**vieille**	**vieil**
fou (mad)	**folle**	**fol**
mou (soft)	**molle**	**mol**
un beau lac a beautiful lake	**une belle vue** a beautiful view	**un bel enfant** a beautiful child
un nouveau **disque** a new record	**la nouvelle année** the new year	**un nouvel ami** a new friend
un vieux tableau an old painting	**la vieille ville** the old town	**un vieil homme** an old man

h) Other irregular feminines:

MASCULINE		FEMININE
favori	(favourite)	**favorite**
gentil	(nice)	**gentille**
nul	(no)	**nulle**
frais	(fresh)	**fraîche**
malin	(shrewd)	**maligne**
sot	(foolish)	**sotte**
long	(long)	**longue**
aigu	(sharp)	**aiguë**
ambigu	(ambiguous)	**ambiguë**
chic	(elegant)	**chic**
châtain	(chestnut)	**châtain**

C. PLURALS OF ADJECTIVES

1. General rule

The masculine and feminine plural of adjectives is formed by adding an s to the singular form:

un vélo neuf
a new bike

des vélos neufs
new bikes

une belle fleur
a beautiful flower

de belles fleurs
beautiful flowers

2. Adjectives ending in 's' or 'x'

If the masculine singular ends in s or x, there is obviously no need to add the s:

il est heureux
he's happy

ils sont heureux
they are happy

un touriste anglais
an English tourist

des touristes anglais
English tourists

3. Others

A few masculine plurals are irregular (the feminine plurals are all regular):

a)

SINGULAR IN -al		PLURAL IN -aux
normal	(normal)	**normaux**
brutal	(brutal)	**brutaux**
loyal	(loyal)	**loyaux**

But:

fatal	(fatal)	**fatals**
final	(final)	**finals**
natal	(native)	**natals**
naval	(naval)	**navals**

b)

SINGULAR IN -eau		PLURAL IN -eaux
beau	(beautiful)	**beaux**
nouveau	(new)	**nouveaux**

D. POSITION OF ADJECTIVES

1. Unlike English adjectives, French adjectives usually follow the noun:

un métier intéressant   **des parents modernes**
an interesting job   modern parents

Adjectives of colour and nationality always follow the noun:

des chaussures rouges   **le drapeau britannique**
red shoes   the British flag

2. However the following common adjectives generally come before the noun:

beau	beautiful
bon	good
court	short
gentil	nice
grand	big, tall
gros	fat
haut	high
jeune	young
joli	pretty
long	long
mauvais	bad
méchant	nasty, naughty (*child*)
meilleur	better
moindre	lesser, least
petit	small
pire	worse
vieux	old
vilain	nasty, ugly

3. Some adjectives have a different meaning according to their position:

	BEFORE NOUN	AFTER NOUN
ancien	former	ancient
brave	good	brave
certain	some	sure
cher	dear	expensive
dernier	last	last (= *latest*)
grand	great (*people only*)	big, tall
même	same	very
pauvre	poor (*pitiable*)	poor (*not rich*)
propre	own	clean
seul	single, only	alone, lonely
simple	mere	simple
vrai	real	true

mon ancien métier my former job	**un tableau ancien** an old painting
un brave type a nice fellow	**un homme brave** a brave man
un certain charme a certain charm	**un fait certain** a definite fact
chère Brigitte dear Brigitte	**un cadeau cher** an expensive present
la dernière séance the last performance	**le mois dernier** last month
une grande vedette a great star	**un homme assez grand** a fairly tall man
le même endroit the same place	**la vérité même** the truth itself
mon pauvre ami ! my poor friend!	**des gens pauvres** poor people
mon propre frère my own brother	**une chambre propre** a clean room
mon seul espoir my only hope	**un homme seul** a lonely man

un simple employé
an ordinary employee

des goûts simples
simple tastes

un vrai casse-pieds
a real bore

une histoire vraie
a true story

4. If a noun is accompanied by several adjectives, the same rules apply to each of them:

le bon vieux temps
the good old days

un joli foulard rouge
a pretty red scarf

E. COMPARATIVE AND SUPERLATIVE OF ADJECTIVES

Persons or things can be compared by using:

1. *the comparative form of the adjective:*

   more ... than, ...er than, less ... than, as ... as

2. *the superlative form of the adjective:*

   the most ... , the ...est, the least ...

1. The comparative

The comparative is formed as follows:

plus ... (que)	**plus long**	**plus cher**
more ...,	longer	more expensive
...er (than)		
moins ... (que)	**moins long**	**moins récent**
less ... than	less long	less recent
aussi ... (que)	**aussi bon**	**aussi important**
as ... (as)	as good	as important

une plus grande maison   **un village plus ancien**
a larger house   an older village

le football est-il plus populaire que le rugby ?
is football more popular than rugby?

ces gants sont moins chauds que les autres
these gloves are less warm than the other ones

elle est beaucoup/bien moins patiente que lui
she's far less patient than he is

le problème de la pollution est tout aussi grave
the pollution problem is just as serious

2. The superlative

a) *Formation*

| le/la/les plus ... | the most ..., the ...est |
| le/la/les moins ... | the least ... |

le plus grand pays
the largest country

la plus grande ville
the largest city

les plus grands acteurs
the greatest actors

les plus grandes voitures
the largest cars

b) *Word order*

i) The normal rules governing word order of adjectives apply. When a superlative adjective comes after the noun, the article is used twice, before the noun and before the adjective:

le plat le plus délicieux
the most delicious dish

l'histoire la plus passionnante
the most exciting story

ii) When a possessive adjective is used, there are two possible constructions, depending on the position of the adjective:

ma plus forte matière
my best subject

or: **son besoin le plus urgent est de trouver un emploi**
his most urgent need is to find a job

c) *'in' is normally translated by* **de:**

la plus jolie maison du quartier/de la ville
the prettiest house in the area/town

le restaurant le plus cher de France
the most expensive restaurant in France

Note: Verbs following the superlative usually take the subjunctive (see p 129).

3. Irregular comparatives and superlatives

ADJECTIVE	COMPARATIVE	SUPERLATIVE
bon good	**meilleur** better	**le meilleur** best
mauvais bad	**pire** **plus mauvais** worse	**le pire** **le plus mauvais** the worst
petit small	**moindre** **plus petit** smaller, lesser	**le moindre** **le plus petit** the smallest, the least

Note: - **plus mauvais** is used in the sense of worse in quality, taste etc

- **moindre** usually means 'less in importance', and **plus petit** means 'less in size':

le moindre de mes soucis
the least of my worries

elle est plus petite que moi
she is smaller than I (am)

5. ADVERBS

Adverbs are normally used with a verb to express:

		ADVERBS OF
how		manner
when		time
where	an action is done	place
with how much intensity		intensity
to what extent		quantity

A. ADVERBS OF MANNER

These are usually formed by adding **-ment** to the adjective (like **-ly** in English):

1. If the adjective ends in a consonant, **-ment** is added to its feminine form:

ADJECTIVE (masc, fem)	ADVERB
doux, douce (soft)	**doucement** (softly)
franc, franche (frank)	**franchement** (frankly)
final, finale (final)	**finalement** (finally)

2. If the adjective ends in a vowel, **-ment** is added to its masculine form:

ADJECTIVE	ADVERB
absolu (absolute)	**absolument** (absolutely)
désespéré (desperate)	**désespérément** (desperately)
vrai (true)	**vraiment** (truly)
simple (simple)	**simplement** (simply)

But: **gai** (cheerful) **gaiement** *or* **gaîment** (cheerfully)

nouveau (new) **nouvellement** (newly)
fou (mad) **follement** (madly)

3. Many adverbs have irregular forms:

a) Some change the **e** of the feminine form of the adjective to **é** before adding **-ment**:

ADJECTIVE	ADVERB
commun (common)	**communément** (commonly)
précis (precise)	**précisément** (precisely)
profond (deep)	**profondément** (deeply)
énorme (enormous)	**énormément** (enormously)
aveugle (blind)	**aveuglément** (blindly)

b) Adjectives which end in **-ent** and **-ant** change to **-emment** and **-amment** *(Note: both endings are pronounced **-amant**)*:

ADJECTIVE	ADVERB
prudent (careful)	**prudemment** (carefully)
évident (obvious)	**évidemment** (obviously)
brillant (brilliant)	**brillamment** (brilliantly)

But: **lent** (slow)   **lentement** (slowly)

4. Some adverbs are completely irregular, including some of the most commonly used ones:

ADJECTIVE	ADVERB
bon (good)	**bien** (well)
bref (brief)	**brièvement** (briefly)
gentil (kind)	**gentiment** (kindly)
mauvais (bad)	**mal** (badly)
meilleur (better)	**mieux** (better)

5. Some adjectives are also used as adverbs in certain set expressions, eg:

parler bas/haut *or* **fort**	to speak softly/loudly
coûter/payer cher	to cost/pay a lot
s'arrêter court	to stop short
couper court	to cut short
voir clair	to see clearly
marcher droit	to walk straight
travailler dur	to work hard
chanter faux/juste	to sing off key/in tune
sentir mauvais/bon	to smell bad/good
refuser net	to refuse point blank

6. After verbs of saying and looking in French an adverbial phrase is often preferred to an adverb, eg:

> **"tu m'écriras ?" dit-il *d'une voix triste***
> "will you write to me?" he said *sadly*

> **elle nous a regardés *d'un air dédaigneux***
> she looked at us *disdainfully*

7. English adverbs may be expressed in French by a preposition followed by a noun, eg:

sans soin	carelessly
avec fierté	proudly
avec amour	lovingly

B.   ADVERBS OF TIME

These are not usually formed from adjectives. Here are the commonest ones:

alors	then
après	afterwards
aujourd'hui	today
aussitôt	at once
bientôt	soon
d'abord	first
déjà	already
demain	tomorrow
encore	still, again
pas encore	not yet
enfin	at last, finally
hier	yesterday
parfois	sometimes
rarement	seldom
souvent	often
tard	late
tôt	early
toujours	always
tout de suite	immediately

c'est déjà Noël !
it's Christmas already!

tu as déjà essayé ?
have you tried before?

il mange encore !
he's still eating!

elle n'est pas encore arrivée
she hasn't arrived yet

C. ADVERBS OF PLACE

Here are the commonest ones:

ailleurs	somewhere else
ici	here
là	there
loin	far away
dessus	on top, on it
au-dessus	over, above
dessous	underneath
au-dessous	below
dedans	inside
dehors	outside
devant	in front, ahead
derrière	behind
partout	everywhere

ne restez pas dehors !
don't stay outside!

mon nom est marqué dessus
my name is written on it

qu'est-ce qu'il y a dedans ?
what's inside?

passez devant
go in front

D. ADVERBS OF INTENSITY AND QUANTITY

These may be used with a verb, an adjective or another adverb. Here are the commonest ones:

à peine	hardly
assez	enough, quite
autant	as much/many
beaucoup	a lot, much/many
combien	how much/many
comme	how
moins	less
plus	more
presque	nearly
peu	little
seulement	only
si	so
tant	so much/many
tellement	so much/many
très	very
trop	too, too much/many
un peu	a little

vous avez assez bu !	**il ne fait pas assez chaud**
you've had enough to drink!	it's not warm enough
nous avons beaucoup ri	**comme c'est amusant !**
we laughed a lot	how funny!
je vais un peu mieux	**c'est si fatigant !**
I'm feeling a little better	it's so tiring!
elle parle trop	**il est très timide**
she talks too much	he's very shy

Note: All of these adverbs, except **à peine**, **comme**, **presque**, **si**, **très**, **seulement**, may be followed by **de** and a noun to express a quantity (see p 219-20).

E. POSITION OF ADVERBS

1. Adverbs usually follow verbs:

> **je vais rarement au théâtre**
> I seldom go to the theatre

> **comme vous conduisez prudemment !**
> you do drive carefully!

2. With compound tenses, shorter adverbs usually come between the auxiliary and the past participle:

> **j'ai enfin terminé**
> I have finished at last

> **il me l'a déjà dit**
> he's already told me

> **nous y sommes souvent allés**
> we've often gone there

> **elle avait beaucoup souffert**
> she had suffered a lot

3. But adverbs of place and many adverbs of time follow the past participle:

> **je l'ai rencontré hier**
> I met him yesterday

> **mettez-le dehors**
> put it outside

> **elle avait cherché partout**
> she had looked everywhere

> **tu t'es couché tard ?**
> did you go to bed late?

4. Adverbs usually come before adjectives or other adverbs:

> **très rarement**
> very seldom

> **elle est vraiment belle**
> she is really beautiful

> **trop vite**
> too quickly

F. COMPARATIVE AND SUPERLATIVE OF ADVERBS

1. The comparative and superlative of adverbs are formed in the same way as adjectives:

ADVERB	COMPARATIVE	SUPERLATIVE
souvent often	**plus souvent (que)** more often (than)	**le plus souvent** (the) most often
	moins souvent (que) less often (than)	**le moins souvent** (the) least often
	aussi souvent (que) as often (as)	

Note: The superlative of the adverb always takes the masculine singular article **le**:

> **je le vois plus souvent qu'avant**
> I see him more often than I used to

> **il conduit moins prudemment que moi**
> he drives less carefully than I do

> **c'est lui qui conduit le moins prudemment**
> he's the one who drives the least carefully

> **je sais cuisiner aussi bien que toi !**
> I can cook as well as you!

Note:

a) **as ... as possible** is translated either by **aussi ... que possible** or by **le plus ... possible**:

> as far as possible   **aussi loin que possible**
>   **le plus loin possible**

b) after a negative, **aussi** is often replaced by **si**:

> **pas si vite !**
> not so fast!

c) In French, the idea of **not so**, **not as** is often expressed by **moins** (less):

> **parle moins fort !**
> don't talk so loud!

2. Irregular comparatives and superlatives

ADVERB	COMPARATIVE	SUPERLATIVE
beaucoup much, a lot	**plus** more	**le plus** (the) most
bien well	**mieux** better	**le mieux** (the) best
mal badly	**pis** *or* **plus mal** worse	**le pis** *or* **le plus mal** (the) worst
peu little	**moins** less	**le moins** (the) least

Note: i) **mieux/le mieux** must not be confused with **meilleur/le meilleur**, which are adjectives, used in front of a noun.

ii) **pis/le pis** are only found in certain set expressions:

tant pis
so much the worse, too bad

de mal en pis
from bad to worse

6. PRONOUNS AND CORRESPONDING ADJECTIVES

A. DEMONSTRATIVES

1. Demonstrative adjectives

a) *CE*

ce is often used to point out a particular person or thing, or persons or things. It is followed by the noun it refers to and agrees in number and gender with that noun:

— with a masculine singular noun: **ce (cet)** this/that
— with a feminine singular noun: **cette** this/that
— with a plural noun (masc or fem): **ces** these/those

ce roman m'a beaucoup plu
I really liked this novel

il a neigé ce matin
it snowed this morning

cette chanson m'énerve
that song gets on my nerves

cette fois, c'est fini !
this time, it's over!

tu trouves que ces lunettes me vont bien ?
do you think these glasses suit me?

cet is used instead of ce in front of a word that begins with a vowel or a silent **h**:

cet après-midi
this afternoon

cet hôtel
that hotel

b) *-CI and -LA*

French does not have separate words to distinguish between 'this' and 'that'. However, when a particular emphasis is being placed on a person or object, or when a contrast is being made between persons or objects, **-ci** and **-là** are added to the noun:

-ci translates the idea of   this/these
-là translates the idea of   that/those

je suis très occupé ces jours-ci
I'm very busy these days

que faisiez-vous ce soir-là ?
what were you doing that evening?

d'où vient ce fromage-là ? — ce fromage-ci, Monsieur ?
where does that cheese come from? — this cheese, sir?

. Demonstrative pronouns

Demonstrative pronouns are used instead of a noun with **ce/cette/ces**.
They are:

a) **celui, celle, ceux, celles**
b) **ce**
c) **ceci, cela, ça**

) *CELUI*

i) **celui** agrees in number and gender with the noun it refers to. It has
four different forms:

	MASCULINE	FEMININE
SINGULAR	celui	celle
PLURAL	ceux	celles

ii) use of **celui**

celui, celle, ceux and **celles** cannot be used on their own. They are
used:

★ with **-ci** or **-là**, for emphasis or for contrast:

celui-ci	celle-ci	this (one)
celui-là	celle-là	that (one)
ceux-ci	celles-ci	these (ones)
ceux-là	celles-là	those (ones)

j'aime bien ce maillot, mais celui-là est moins cher
I like this swimsuit, but that one is cheaper

je voudrais ces fleurs — lesquelles ? celles-ci ou celles-là ?
I'd like these flowers — which ones? these or those?

★ with **de** + noun, to express possession:

je préfère mon ordinateur à celui de Jean-Claude
I prefer my computer to Jean-Claude's

range ta chambre plutôt que celle de ta sœur
tidy your own bedroom rather than your sister's

mes parents sont moins sévères que ceux de Nicole
my parents aren't as strict as Nicole's

les douches municipales sont mieux que celles du camping
the public showers are better than those at the campsite

★ with the relative pronouns **qui**, **que**, **dont** to introduce a relative
   clause (for use of these relative pronouns, see p 85-90).

celui/celle/ceux/celles qui	the one(s) who/which
celui/celle/ceux/celles que	the one(s) whom/which
celui/celle/ceux/celles dont	the one(s) of which/whose

lequel est ton père ? celui qui a une moustache ?
which one is your father? the one with the moustache?

regarde cette voiture ! celle qui est garée au coin
look at that car! the one which is parked at the corner

deux filles, celles qu'il avait rencontrées la veille
two girls, the ones he had met the day before

voilà mon copain, celui dont je t'ai parlé l'autre jour
here's my friend, the one I told you about the other day

b) *CE*

i) **ce** (meaning 'it', 'that') is mostly found with the verb **être**:

c'est	**ce serait**	**c'était**
it's/that's	it/that would be	it/that was

Note: **ce** changes to **c'** before an **e** or an **é**.

ii) use of **ce**

★ with a noun or pronoun, **ce** is used to identify people or things, or to
   emphasize them; it is translated in a variety of ways:

qu'est-ce que c'est ? — c'est mon billet d'avion
what's that? — it's my plane ticket

qui est-ce ? — c'est moi   **ce doit être lui**
who is it? — it's me   that must be him

c'est un artiste bien connu   **c'était une bonne idée**
he's a well-known artist   it was a good idea

ce sont mes amis
they're my friends

c'est elle qui l'a fait
she's the one who did it

c'est la dernière fois !
it's the last time!

c'est celui que j'ai vu
he's the one I saw

★ before an adjective, **ce** is used to refer to an idea, an event or a fact which has already been mentioned; it does not refer to any specific noun:

c'était formidable
it was great

oui, c'est vrai
yes, that's true

ce n'est pas grave
it doesn't matter
or it's not serious

ce serait amusant
it would be funny

c'est sûr ?
is that definite?

c'est bon à entendre
that's good to hear

Note: the translation of **it** is an area of some difficulty for students of French, as it is sometimes translated by **ce** and sometimes by **il/elle**; see p 242-3.

c) CECI, CELA, ÇA

ceci (this), **cela** (that) and **ça** (that) are used to refer to an idea, an event, a fact or an object. They never refer to a particular noun already mentioned.

non, je n'aime pas ça !
no, I don't like that!

ça, c'est un acteur !
that's what I call an actor!

ça m'est égal
I don't mind

buvez ceci, ça vous fera du bien
drink this, it'll do you good

ça alors !
well, really!

cela s'appelle comment, en anglais ?
what do you call this in English?

ah, bon ? cela m'étonne
really? that surprises me

souvenez-vous de ceci
remember this

cela ne vous regarde pas
that's none of your business

Note: **ceci** is not very common in French; **cela** and **ça** are often used to translate 'this' as well as 'that'; **ça** is used far more frequently than **cela** in spoken French.

B. INDEFINITE ADJECTIVES AND PRONOUNS

1. Indefinite adjectives

They are:

MASCULINE	FEMININE	
autre(s)	**autre(s)**	other
certain(s)	**certaine(s)**	certain
chaque	**chaque**	each, every
même(s)	**même(s)**	same
plusieurs	**plusieurs**	several
quelque(s)	**quelque(s)**	some
tel(s)	**telle(s)**	such
tout (tous)	**toute(s)**	all, every

a) *CHAQUE and PLUSIEURS*

chaque (each) is always singular, **plusieurs** (several) always plural; the feminine form is the same as the masculine form:

j'y vais chaque jour	**chaque personne**
I go there every day	each person
plusieurs années	**il a plusieurs amis**
several years	he's got several friends

b) *AUTRE, MEME and QUELQUE*

autre (other), **même** (same) and **quelque** (some) agree in number with the noun that follows; the feminine is the same as the masculine:

je voudrais un autre café	**d'autres couleurs**
I'd like another coffee	other colours
la même taille	**les mêmes touristes**
the same size	the same tourists
quelque temps après	**à quelques kilomètres**
some time later	a few kilometres away

Note: **même** has a different meaning when placed after the noun (see p 42).

c) *CERTAIN, TEL and TOUT*

certain (certain, some), **tel** (such) and **tout** (all) agree in number and gender with the noun; they have four different forms:

un certain charme a certain charm	**une certaine dame** a certain lady
à certains moments at (certain) times	**certaines personnes** some people
un tel homme such a man	**une telle aventure** such an adventure
de tels avantages such advantages	**de telles difficultés** such difficulties

quoi ! tu as mangé tout le fromage et tous les fruits ?
what! you've eaten all the cheese and all the fruit?

toute la journée all day long	**toutes mes matières** all my subjects

Note:

i) **tel**: the position of the article **un/une** with **tel** is not the same as in English: **un tel homme** = such a man.

ii) **tel** cannot qualify another adjective; when it is used as an adverb, 'such' is translated by **si** or **tellement** (so):

c'était un si bon repas/un repas tellement bon !
it was such a good meal!

iii) **tous les/toutes les** are often translated by 'every':

tous les jours every day	**toutes les places** all seats, every seat

2. Indefinite pronouns

a) These are:

MASC	FEM	
aucun	aucune	none, not any
autre(s)	autre(s)	another one, other ones
certains	certaine(s)	certain, some
chacun	chacune	each one, everyone
on		one, someone, you, they, people, we
personne		nobody
plusieurs	plusieurs	several (ones)
quelque chose		something, anything
quelqu'un		someone
quelques-uns	quelques-unes	some, a few
rien		nothing
tout (tous)	toute(s)	everything, every one, all

pas celui-là, l'autre
not that one, the other one

où sont les autres ?
where are the others?

certains disent que ...
some say that...

personne n'est venu
no one came

qui est là ? — personne
who's there? — nobody

qu'as-tu ? — rien
what's wrong? — nothing

plusieurs d'entre eux
several of them

chacun pour soi !
every man for himself!

il manque quelque chose ?
is anything missing?

dis quelque chose !
say something!

quelqu'un l'a averti
someone warned him

il y a quelqu'un ?
is anyone in?

j'ai tout oublié
I've forgotten everything

c'est tout, merci
that's all, thanks

elles sont toutes arrivées
they've all arrived

allons-y tous ensemble
let's all go together

b) *Points to note*

i) **aucun(e)**, **personne** and **rien**: these can be used on their own, but they are more often used with a verb and the negative word **ne** (see negative expressions, p 229-31):

    personne n'habite ici   **il n'y a rien à manger**
    no one lives here   there's nothing to eat

ii) **aucun(e)**, **un(e) autre**, **d'autres**, **certain(e)s**, **plusieurs** and **quelques-un(e)s**: when these pronouns are used as direct objects, the pronoun **en** must be used before the verb:

    je n'en ai lu aucun   **donne-m'en une autre**
    I haven't read any (of them)   give me another one

    j'en ai vu d'autres qui étaient moins chers
    I saw other ones which were cheaper

    j'en connais certains   **il y en a plusieurs**
    I know some of them   there are several

    tu m'en donnes quelques-   **achètes-en quelques-unes**
    uns ?   buy a few
    will you give me a few?

iii) **personne**, **quelque chose**, **rien**, **plusieurs**: when these are followed by an adjective, the preposition **de (d')** must be used in front of the adjective:

    il n'y a personne de libre   **quelque chose de mieux**
    there's no one available   something better

    il y en avait plusieurs de   **rien de grave**
    cassés   nothing serious
    several of them were broken

iv) **autre** is commonly used in the following expressions:

    quelqu'un d'autre   **quelque chose**   **rien d'autre**
    someone else   **d'autre**   nothing else
        something else

c) *ON*

This pronoun is used in a variety of ways in French. It can mean:

i) *one/you/they/people* in a general sense:

en France, on roule à droite
in France, they drive on the right

on ne sait jamais   **on ne doit pas mentir**
you/one never know(s)   you shouldn't lie

ii) *someone* (an undefined person)

In this sense, **on** is often translated by the passive (see p 150):

on me l'a déjà dit   **on vous l'apportera**
someone's already told me   someone will bring you it
I've already been told   it will be brought to you

iii) *we*

In spoken French, **on** is increasingly used instead of **nous**; although it refers to a plural subject, it is followed by the third person singular:

qu'est-ce qu'on fait ?   **fais vite, on t'attend !**
what shall we do?   hurry up, we're waiting for you!

Note: in compound tenses with the auxiliary **être**, the agreement of the past participle with **on** is optional:

on est allé au cinéma   **on est rentré en taxi**
on est allés au cinéma   **on est rentrées en taxi**
we went to the pictures   we got home by taxi

C. INTERROGATIVE AND EXCLAMATORY ADJECTIVES AND PRONOUNS

1. The interrogative adjective QUEL ?

a) *Forms*

quel (which, what) agrees in number and gender with the noun it refers to. It has four forms:

— with a masc sing noun: **quel ?**
— with a fem sing noun: **quelle ?**
— with a masc plur noun: **quels ?**
— with a fem plur noun: **quelles ?**

b) *Direct questions:*

quel est votre passe-temps favori ?
what's your favourite pastime?

quelle heure est-il ?
what time is it?

quels jours as-tu de libres ?
which days have you got free?

quelles affaires comptes-tu prendre avec toi ?
what/which things do you intend to take with you?

c) *Indirect questions:*

je ne sais pas quel disque choisir
I don't know which record to choose

il se demande quelle veste lui va le mieux
he's wondering which jacket suits him best

2. The exclamatory adjective QUEL !

quel ! has the same forms as the interrogative adjective **quel ?**:

quel dommage !   **quelle belle maison !**
what a pity!   what a beautiful house!

quels imbéciles !
what idiots!

3. Interrogative pronouns

These are:

lequel/laquelle/	which (one(s))?
lesquel(le)s ?	
qui ?	who?, whom?
que ?	what?
quoi ?	what?
ce qui	what
ce que	what

ce qui and **ce que** are used only in indirect questions; all other interrogative pronouns can be used both in direct and indirect questions.

a) *LEQUEL ?*

i) forms

lequel (which?, which one?) agrees in gender and in number with the noun it stands for:

— with a masc sing noun:	**lequel ?**	which (one)?
— with a fem sing noun:	**laquelle ?**	which (one)?
— with a masc plur noun:	**lesquels ?**	which (ones)?
— with a fem plur noun:	**lesquelles ?**	which (ones)?

after the prepositions **à** and **de**, the following changes occur:

à + lequel ?	→	**auquel ?**
à + lesquels ?	→	**auxquels ?**
à + lesquelles ?	→	**auxquelles ?**
de + lequel ?	→	**duquel ?**
de + lesquels ?	→	**desquels ?**
de + lesquelles ?	→	**desquelles ?**

à/de + laquelle ? do not change

ii) direct questions:

je cherche un hôtel ; lequel recommandez-vous ?
I'm looking for a hotel; which one do you recommend?

nous avons plusieurs couleurs ; vous préférez laquelle ?
we have several colours; which one do you prefer?

lesquels de ces livres sont à toi ?
which of these books are yours?

je voudrais essayer ces chaussures — lesquelles ?
I would like to try these shoes on — which ones?

iii) indirect questions:

demande-lui lequel de ces ordinateurs est le moins cher
ask him which (one) of these computers is the cheapest

c'est dans une de ces rues, mais je ne sais plus laquelle
it's in one of these streets, but I can't remember which one

QUI ?

qui (who?, whom?) is used to refer to people; it can be both subject and object and can be used after a preposition:

qui t'a accompagné ?   **qui as-tu appelé ?**
who accompanied you?   who did you call?

tu y vas avec qui ?   **c'est pour qui ?**
who are you going with?   who is it for?

pour qui vous prenez-vous ?   **à qui l'as-tu donné ?**
who do you think you are?   who did you give it to?

Note: **que** (not **qui**!) changes to **qu'** before a vowel or a silent **h**:

qui est-ce qu'elle attend ?
who is she waiting for?

qui ? can be replaced by **qui est-ce qui ?** (subject) or **qui est-ce que ?** (object) in direct questions:

qui est-ce qui veut du café ?   **qui est-ce que tu as vu ?**
who wants coffee?   who did you see?

avec qui est-ce que tu sors ce soir ?
who are you going out with tonight?

But: **qui** cannot be replaced by **qui est-ce qui** or **qui est-ce que** in indirect questions:

j'aimerais savoir qui vous a dit ça
I'd like to know who told you that

elle se demandait de qui étaient les fleurs
she was wondering who the flowers were from

For more details on the use of **qui/que** as relative pronouns, see p 85-90.

c) *QUE ?*

que (what?) is used to refer to things; it is only used in direct questions; it is always a direct object and cannot be used after prepositions:

que désirez-vous ?   **qu'a-t-il dit ?**
what do you wish?   what did he say?

que ? is rather formal and is usually replaced by **qu'est-ce qui** or **qu'est-ce que ?** in spoken French.

Note: **que** becomes **qu'** before a vowel or a silent **h**.

d) *QU'EST-CE QUI ?*

qu'est-ce qui ? (what?) is used as the subject of a verb; it cannot refer to a person:

qu'est-ce qui lui est arrivé ?
what happened to him?

qu'est-ce qui la fait rire ?
what makes her laugh?

e) *QU'EST-CE QUE ?*

qu'est-ce que ? (what?) replaces **que ?** as the object of a verb; it becomes **qu'est-ce qu'** before a vowel or a silent **h**:

qu'est-ce que tu aimes lire ?
what do you like reading?

qu'est-ce qu'il va faire pendant les vacances ?
what's he going to do during the holidays?

f) *QUOI ?*

quoi ? (what?) refers to things; it is used:

i) instead of **que** or **qu'est-ce que** after a preposition:

à quoi penses-tu ?   **dans quoi l'as-tu mis ?**
what are you thinking about?   what did you put it in?

ii) in indirect questions:

demandez-lui de quoi il a besoin
ask him what he needs

je ne sais pas à quoi ça sert
I don't know what it's for

g) *CE QUI, CE QUE*

ce qui and ce que (what) are only used in indirect questions; they
replace qu'est-ce qui and (qu'est-ce) que.

They are used in the same way as the relative pronouns **ce qui** and **ce
que** (see p 89-90).

i) ce qui is used as the subject of the verb in the indirect question (ce
qui is the subject of s'est passé in the following example):

> **nous ne saurons jamais ce qui s'est passé**
> we'll never know what happened

ii) **ce que**

ce que (ce qu' before a vowel or a silent h) is used as the object of the
verb in the indirect question (ce que is the object of il faisait in the
following example):

> **je n'ai pas remarqué ce qu'il faisait**
> I didn't notice what he was doing

D. PERSONAL PRONOUNS

There are four categories of personal pronouns:

— **subject** pronouns
— **object** pronouns
— **disjunctive** pronouns
— **reflexive** pronouns

For reflexive pronouns, see p 109-10.

1. Subject pronouns

PERSON	SINGULAR		PLURAL	
1st	**je (j')**	I	**nous**	we
2nd	**tu**	you	**vous**	you
3rd	**il**	he, it	**ils**	they
	elle	she, it	**elles**	they
	on	one, we, they		

Note:

a) **je** changes to **j'** before a vowel or a silent **h**:

j'ai honte   **j'adore les frites**
I'm ashamed   I love chips

j'habite en Ecosse
I live in Scotland

b) **tu** and **vous**

vous can be plural or singular; it is used when speaking to more than one person (plural), or to a stranger or an older person (singular):

vous venez, les gars ?   **vous parlez l'anglais, Monsieur ?**
are you coming, lads?   do you speak English (, sir)?

tu is used when speaking to a friend, a relative, a younger person, or someone you know well:

tu viens, Marc ?
are you coming, Marc?

c) **il/ils, elle/elles** may refer to people, animals or things, and must be of the same gender as the noun they replace:

> **ton stylo ?** *il* **est là**
> your pen? there *it* is
>
> **ta montre ?** *elle* **est là**
> your watch? there *it* is
>
> **tes gants ?** *ils* **sont là**
> your gloves? there *they* are
>
> **tes lunettes ?** *elles* **sont là**
> your glasses? there *they* are

When referring to several nouns of different genders, French uses the masculine plural **ils**:

> **tu as vu** *le* **stylo et** *la* **montre de Marie? — oui,** *ils* **sont dans son sac**
> have you seen Marie's pen and watch? — yes, *they*'re in her bag

d) **on**: see p 64.

2. Object pronouns

These include:
— direct object pronouns
— indirect object pronouns
— the pronouns **en** and **y**

a) *Forms*

	PERSON	DIRECT	INDIRECT
SING	1st	**me (m')** me	**me (m')** (to) me
	2nd	**te (t')** you	**te (t')** (to) you
	3rd	**le (l')** him, it	**lui** (to) him
		la (l') her, it	**lui** (to) her
PLUR	1st	**nous** us	**nous** (to) us
	2nd	**vous** you	**vous** (to) you
	3rd	**les** them	**leur** (to) them

Note:

i) **me**, **te**, **le** and **la** change to **m'**, **t'** and **l'** before a vowel or a silent **h**:

il m'énerve !	**je m'habituerai à lui**
he gets on my nerves!	I'll get used to him

ii) **te** and **vous**: the same distinction should be made as between the subject pronouns **tu** and **vous** (see p 70).

iii) **le**: is sometimes used in an impersonal sense, when it refers to a fact, a statement or an idea which has already been expressed; it is usually not translated in English:

j'irai en Amérique un jour ; en tout cas je *l'*espère
I'll go to America one day; I hope so anyway

elle a eu un bébé — je *le* sais, elle me *l'*a dit
she's had a baby — I know, she told me

iv) **moi** and **toi** are used instead of **me** and **te**, except when **en** follows:

écris-*moi* bientôt	**donne *m'*en**
write to me soon	give me some

b) *Position*

In French, object pronouns come immediately before the verb they refer to. With a compound tense, they come before the auxiliary:

on *t'*attendra ici	**je *l'*ai rencontrée en ville**
we'll wait for you here	I met her in town

Note: When there are two verbs, the pronoun comes immediately before the verb it refers to:

j'aimerais lui demander	**tu *l'*as entendu chanter ?**
I'd like to ask him	have you heard him sing?

In positive commands (affirmative imperative) the pronoun follows the verb and is joined to it by a hyphen:

regarde-*les* !	**parle-*lui* !**
look at them!	speak to him!

dis-*nous* ce qui s'est passé
tell us what happened

c) *Direct pronouns and indirect pronouns*

i) Direct object pronouns replace a noun which follows the verb directly. They answer the question 'who(m)?' or 'what'?

WHO(M) did you see?	I saw *my friend*; I saw *him*
qui as-tu vu ?	**j'ai vu *mon ami* ; je *l'*ai vu**
tu *me* connais	**j'aime *le* voir danser**
you know *me*	I like to see *him* dance
je *les* ai trouvés	**ne *nous* ennuie pas !**
I found *them*	don't bother *us!*

ii) Indirect object pronouns replace a noun which follows the verb with a linking preposition (usually **à** = 'to'). They answer the question 'who(m) to?':

WHO did you speak to?	I spoke *to Marc*; I spoke *to him*
à qui as-tu parlé ?	**j'ai parlé *à Marc* ; je *lui* ai parlé**
elle *lui* a menti	**je *te* donne ce disque**
she lied *to him*	I'm giving this record *to you*
je ne *leur* parle plus	
I'm not talking *to them* any more	

iii) **le/la/les** or **lui/leur** ?

Direct pronouns differ from indirect pronouns only in the 3rd person and great care must be taken here:

★ English indirect object pronouns often look like direct objects; this becomes obvious when the object is placed at the end of the sentence:

I showed him your photo = I showed your photo to him
je *lui* ai montré ta photo

This is particularly the case with the following verbs:

acheter	to buy	**offrir**	to offer
donner	to give	**prêter**	to lend
montrer	to show	**vendre**	to sell

je *lui* ai acheté un livre	**ne *leur* prête pas mes affaires**
I bought him a book	don't lend them my things
= I bought a book *for him*	= don't lend my things *to them*

★ Some verbs take a direct object in English and an indirect object in French (see p 193):

> **je ne *lui* ai rien dit**
> I didn't tell *him* anything
>
> **je *leur* demanderai**
> I'll ask *them*
>
> **tu *lui* ressembles**
> you look like *him*
>
> **téléphone-*leur***
> phone *them*

★ Some verbs take a direct object in French and an indirect object in English (see p 192):

> **je *l'*attends**
> I'm waiting *for him*
>
> **écoutez-*les* !**
> listen *to them*!

d) *Order of object pronouns*

When several object pronouns are used together, they come in the following order:

i) Before the verb:

1	**me**	**te**	**nous**	**vous**
2	**le**	**la**	**les**	
3		**lui**	**leur**	

> **il *me l'*a donné**
> he gave me it
>
> **je vais *vous les* envoyer**
> I'll send them to you
>
> **ne *la leur* vends pas**
> don't sell it to them
>
> **je *le lui* ai acheté**
> I bought it for him

ii) After the verb:

With a positive command (affirmative imperative), the order is as follows:

1		**le**	**la**		**les**
2	**moi (m')**	**toi (t')**		**nous**	**vous**
3		**lui**	**leur**		

> **apporte-*les-moi* !**
> bring them to me!
>
> **prête-*la-nous* !**
> lend us it!
>
> **dites-*le lui* !**
> tell him!
>
> **rends-*la leur* !**
> give it back to them!

3. The pronoun *EN*

a) *Use*

en is used instead of **de** + noun. Since **de** has a variety of meanings, **en** can be used in a number of ways:

i) It means 'of it/them', but also 'with it/them', 'about it/them', 'from it/there', 'out of it/there':

tu es sûr *du prix* ? — j'*en* suis sûr
are you sure of the price? — I'm sure *of it*

je suis content *de ce cadeau* ; j'*en* suis content
I'm pleased with this present; I'm pleased *with it*

elle est folle *des animaux* ; elle *en* est folle
she's crazy about animals; she's crazy *about them*

il est descendu *du train* ; il *en* est descendu
he got off the train; he got *off it*

il revient *de Paris* ; il *en* revient
he's coming back from Paris; he's coming *from there*

ii) Verb constructions

Particular care should be taken with verbs and expressions which are followed by **de** + noun. Since **de** is not always translated in the same way, **en** may have a number of meanings:

il a envie *de ce livre* ; il *en* a envie
he wants this book; he wants *it*

je te remercie *de ta carte* ; je t'*en* remercie
I thank you for your card; I thank you *for it*

tu as besoin *de ces papiers* ? tu *en* as besoin ?
do you need these papers? do you need *them?*

elle a peur *des chiens* ; elle *en* a peur
she's afraid of dogs; she's afraid *of them*

tu te souviens *de ce film* ? tu t'*en* souviens ?
do you remember this film? do you remember *it*?

iii) 'some'/'any'

en replaces the partitive article (**du, de la, des**) + noun; it means 'some'/'any':

> **tu veux *du café* ? — non, je n'*en* veux pas**
> do you want (any) coffee? — no, I don't want *any*

> **j'achète *des fruits* ? — non, j'*en* ai chez moi**
> shall I buy (some) fruit? — no, I've got *some* at home

> **il y a *de la place* ? — *en* voilà là-bas**
> is there any room? — there's some over there

iv) Expressions of quantity

en must be used with expressions of quantity not followed by a noun. It replaces **de** + noun and means 'of it/them', but is seldom translated in English:

> **tu as pris assez *d'argent* ? tu *en* as pris assez ?**
> did you take enough money? did you take enough?

> **vous avez *combien de frères* ? — j'*en* ai deux**
> how many brothers do you have? — I've got two

> **j'ai fini *mes cigarettes* ; je vais *en* acheter un paquet**
> I've finished my cigarettes; I'm going to buy a packet

b) *Position*

Like object pronouns, **en** comes immediately before the verb, except with positive commands (affirmative imperative), where it comes after the verb and is linked to it by a hyphen:

j'*en* veux un kilo I want a kilo (of it/them)	**j'*en* ai marre !** I'm fed up (with it)!
prends-*en* assez ! take enough (of it/them)!	**laisses-*en* aux autres !** leave some for the others!

When used in conjunction with other object pronouns, it always comes last:

ne *m'en* parlez pas ! don't tell me about it!	**je *vous en* donnerai** I'll give you some
prête-*lui-en* ! lend him some!	**gardez-*nous-en* !** keep some for us!

4. The pronoun Y

a) Use

y is used instead of **à** + noun (not referring to a person). It is used:

i) As the indirect object of a verb. Since the preposition **à** is translated in a variety of ways in English, **y** may have various meanings (it, of it/them, about it/them etc):

tu joues *au tennis* ? — non, j'y joue rarement
do you play tennis? — no, I seldom play (*it*)

je pense *à mes examens* ; j'y pense souvent
I'm thinking *about* my exams; I often think *about them*

il s'intéresse *à la photo* ; il s'y intéresse
he's interested in photography; he's interested *in it*

ii) Meaning 'there':

j'ai passé deux jours *à Londres* ; j'y ai passé deux jours
I spent two days in London; I spent two days there

il est allé *en Grèce* ; il y est allé
he went to Greece; he went there

Note: y must always be used with the verb **aller** (to go) when the place is not mentioned in the clause. It is often not translated in English:

comment vas-tu *à l'école* ? — j'y vais en bus
how do you go to school? — I go (there) by bus

allons-y !   **on y va demain**
let's go!   we're going (there) tomorrow

iii) Replacing the prepositions **en**, **dans**, **sur** + noun; y then means 'there', 'in it/them', 'on it/them':

je voudrais vivre *en France* ; je voudrais y vivre
I'd like to live in France; I'd like to live *there*

je les ai mis *dans ma poche* ; je les y ai mis
I put them in my pocket; I put them *there*

***sur la table* ? non, je ne l'y vois pas**
on the table? no, I don't see it *there*

b) *Position*

Like other object pronouns, **y** comes immediately before the verb, except with a positive command (affirmative imperative), where it must follow the verb:

j'y réfléchirai	**il s'y est habitué**
I'll think about it	he got used to it
pensez-y !	**n'y allez pas !**
think about it!	don't go!

When used with other object pronouns, **y** comes last:

il va *nous* **y rencontrer**	**je** *l'***y ai vu hier**
he'll meet us there	I saw him there yesterday

5. Disjunctive pronouns

a) *Forms*

PERSON	SINGULAR	PLURAL
1st	**moi**	**nous**
	me	us
2nd	**toi**	**vous**
	you	you
3rd (masc)	**lui**	**eux**
	him	them
(fem)	**elle**	**elles**
	her	them
(impersonal)	**soi**	
	oneself	

Note:

i) **toi/vous**: the same difference should be made as between **tu** and **vous** (see p 70).

ii) **soi** is used in an impersonal, general sense to refer to indefinite pronouns and adjectives (**on**, **chacun**, **tout le monde**, **personne**, **chaque** etc); it is mainly found in set phrases, such as:

    chacun pour soi
    every man for himself

b) *Use*

Disjunctive pronouns, also called emphatic pronouns, are used instead of object pronouns (only when referring to persons) in the following cases:

i) In answer to a question, alone or in a phrase without a verb:

qui est là ? — moi
who's there? — me

j'aime les pommes ; et toi ?
I like apples; do you?

qui préfères-tu, lui ou elle ? — elle, bien sûr
who do you prefer, him or her? — her, of course

ii) After **c'est/ce sont, c'était/étaient** etc:

ouvrez, c'est moi !
open up, it's me!

non, ce n'était pas lui
no, it wasn't him

iii) After a preposition:

vous allez chez lui ?
are you going to his place?

tu y vas avec elle ?
are you going with her?

regarde devant toi !
look in front of you!

oh, c'est pour moi ?
oh, is that for me?

iv) Verb constructions: special care should be taken with verbs followed by a preposition:

tu peux compter sur moi
you can count on me

quoi ! tu as peur de lui ?
what! you're afraid of him?

il m'a parlé de toi
he told me about you

je pense souvent à vous
I often think about you

Note: Emphatic pronouns are only used when referring to persons. Otherwise, use **y** or **en**.

v) For emphasis, particularly when two pronouns are contrasted. The unstressed subject pronoun is usually included:

vous, vous m'énervez !
you get on my nerves!

lui, il joue bien ; elle, non
he plays well; *she* doesn't

moi, je n'aime pas l'hiver
I don't like winter

eux, ils sont partis
they've left

vi) In the case of multiple subjects (two pronouns or one pronoun and one noun):

lui et son frère sont dans l'équipe
he and his brother are in the team

ma famille et moi allons très bien
my family and I are very well

vii) As the second term of comparisons:

il est plus sympa que toi   **elle chante mieux que lui**
he is nicer than you   she sings better than he does

viii) Before a relative pronoun:

c'est lui que j'aime   **c'est toi qui l'as dit**
he's the one I love   you're the one who said it

lui qui n'aime pas le vin blanc en a bu six verres
he, who doesn't like white wine, had six glasses

ix) With **-même(s)** (-self, -selves), **aussi** (too), **seul** (alone):

faites-le vous-mêmes   **j'irai moi-même**
do it yourselves   I'll go myself

lui aussi est parti   **elle seule le sait**
he too went away   she alone knows

x) To replace a possessive pronoun (see p 84):

c'est *le mien* ; il est à moi
it's mine; it belongs to me

E. POSSESSIVE ADJECTIVES AND PRONOUNS

1. Possessive adjectives

a) *Forms*

Possessive adjectives always come before a noun. Like other adjectives, they agree in gender and number with the noun; the masculine and feminine plural are identical:

SINGULAR		PLURAL	
MASC	FEM		
mon	ma	mes	my
ton	ta	tes	your
son	sa	ses	his/her/its/one's
notre	notre	nos	our
votre	votre	vos	your
leur	leur	leurs	their

j'ai mis mon argent et mes affaires dans mon sac
I've put my money and my things in my bag

comment va ton frère ? et ta sœur ? et tes parents ?
how's your brother? and your sister? and your parents?

notre rue est assez calme   **ce sont vos amis**
our street is fairly quiet   they're your friends

Note: **mon/ton/son** are used instead of **ma/ta/sa** when the next word starts with a vowel or silent **h**:

mon ancienne maison   **ton amie Christine**
my old house   your friend Christine

son haleine sentait l'alcool
his breath smelled of alcohol

b) *Use*

i) The possessive adjective is repeated before each noun and agrees with it:

mon père et ma mère sont sortis
my mother and father have gone out

ii) **son/sa/ses**

son, sa and **ses** can all mean 'his', 'her' or 'its'. In French, the form of the adjective is determined by the gender and number of the noun that follows, and not by the possessor:

> **il m'a prêté sa mobylette et son casque**
> he lent me his moped and his helmet

> **elle s'entend bien avec sa mère, mais pas avec son père**
> she gets on well with her mother, but not with her father

> **il cire ses chaussures ; elle repasse ses chemisiers**
> he's polishing his shoes; she's ironing her shirts

iii) **ton/ta/tes** and **votre/vos**

The two sets of words for 'your', **ton/ta/tes** and **votre/vos**, correspond to the two different forms **tu** and **vous**; they must not be used together with the same person:

> **Papa, tu as parlé à ton patron ?**
> have you spoken to your boss, Dad?

> **Monsieur ! votre brochure ! vous ne la prenez pas ?**
> Sir! your brochure! aren't you taking it?

iv) In French, the possessive adjective is replaced by the definite article (**le/la/les**) with the following:

★ parts of the body:

> **il s'est essuyé les mains**   **elle a haussé les épaules**
> he wiped his hands   she shrugged (her shoulders)

★ descriptive phrases tagged on to the end of a clause, where English adds 'with':

> **il marchait lentement, les main dans les poches**
> he was walking slowly, with his hands in his pockets

> **elle l'a regardé partir les larmes aux yeux**
> she watched him leave with tears in her eyes

2. Possessive pronouns

MASC	FEM	PLURAL (MASC AND FEM)	
le mien	la mienne	les mien(ne)s	mine
le tien	la tienne	les tien(ne)s	yours
le sien	la sienne	les sien(ne)s	his/hers/its
le nôtre	la nôtre	les nôtres	ours
le vôtre	la vôtre	les vôtres	yours
le leur	la leur	les leurs	theirs

Possessive pronouns are used intead of a possessive adjective + noun. They agree in gender and in number with the noun they stand for, and not with the possessor (it is particularly important to remember this when translating 'his' and 'hers'):

j'aime bien ton chapeau, mais je préfère le mien
I quite like your hat, but I prefer mine

on prend quelle voiture ? la mienne ou la tienne ?
which car shall we take? mine or yours?

comment sont vos profs ? les nôtres sont sympas
what are your teachers like? ours are nice

j'ai pris mon passeport, mais Brigitte a oublié le sien
I brought my passport, but Brigitte forgot hers

j'ai gardé ma moto, mais Paul a vendu la sienne
I've kept my motorbike but Paul has sold his

à or de + possessive pronoun

The prepositions **à** or **de** combine with the articles **le** and **les** in the usual way:

à + le mien	→	au mien
à + les miens	→	aux miens
à + les miennes	→	aux miennes
de + le mien	→	du mien
de + les miens	→	des miens
de + les miennes	→	des miennes

demande à tes parents, j'ai déjà parlé aux miens
ask your parents, I've already spoken to mine

leur appartement ressemble beaucoup au nôtre
their flat is very similar to ours

j'aime bien les chiens, mais j'ai peur du tien
I like dogs, but I'm afraid of yours

Note: after the verb **être**, the possessive pronoun is often replaced by **à** + emphatic (disjunctive) pronoun (see p 80):

à qui est cette écharpe ? — elle est à moi
whose scarf is this? — it's mine

ce livre est à toi ? — non, il est à elle
is this book yours? — no, it's hers

c'est à qui ? à vous ou à lui ?
whose is this? yours or his?

F. RELATIVE PRONOUNS

1. Definition

Relative pronouns are words which introduce a relative clause. In the following sentence:

I bought the book which you recommended

'which' is the relative pronoun, 'which you recommended' is the relative clause and 'the book' is the antecedent (ie the noun the relative pronoun refers to).

2. Forms

Relative pronouns are:

qui	who, which	**lequel**	which
que	who(m), which	**dont**	of which, whose
quoi	what	**ce qui**	what
où	where	**ce que**	what

qui, **que**, **quoi**, **lequel**, **ce qui** and **ce que** can also be used as interrogative pronouns (see p 66-9) and must not be confused with them.

3. Use

a) *QUI*

qui is used as the subject of a relative clause; it means:

i) 'who', 'that' (referring to people):

connaissez-vous le monsieur qui habite ici ?
do you know the man who lives here?

ce n'est pas lui qui a menti
he's not the one who lied

ii) 'which', 'that' (referring to things):

tu as pris le journal qui était sur la télé ?
did you take the paper which/that was on the telly?

b) *QUE*

que (written **qu'** before a vowel or a silent **h**) is used as the object of a relative clause; it is often not translated and means:

i) 'who(m)', 'that' (referring to people):

la fille que j'aime ne m'aime pas
the girl (that) I love doesn't love me

ii) 'which', 'that' (referring to things):

j'ai perdu le briquet qu'il m'a offert
I've lost the lighter (which/that) he gave me

c) *qui* or *que*?

qui (subject) and **que** (object) are translated by the same words in English (who, which, that). To use the correct pronoun in French, it is essential to know whether a relative pronoun is the object or the subject of the relative clause:

i) when the verb of the relative clause has its own subject, the object pronoun **que** must be used:

c'est un passse-temps que j'adore
it's a pastime (that) *I* love (*the subject of 'adore' is 'je'*)

ii) otherwise the relative pronoun is the subject of the verb in the relative clause and the subject pronoun **qui** must be used:

j'ai trouvé un manteau qui me plaît
I found a coat that I like (*the subject of 'plaît' is 'qui'*)

d) *LEQUEL*

i) forms

lequel (which) has four different forms, as it must agree with the noun it refers to:

	SINGULAR	PLURAL	
MASCULINE	**lequel**	**lesquels**	} which
FEMININE	**laquelle**	**lesquelles**	

lequel etc combines with the prepositions **à** and **de** as follows:

à + lequel	→	**auquel**
à + lesquels	→	**auxquels**
à + lesquelles	→	**auxquelles**
de + lequel	→	**duquel**
de + lesquels	→	**desquels**
de + lesquelles	→	**desquelles**

à + laquelle and **de + laquelle** do not change.

quels sont les sports auxquels tu t'intéresses ?
what are the sports (which) you are interested *in*?

voilà le village près duquel on campait
here's the village near which we camped

ii) qui or lequel with a preposition?

When a relative pronoun follows a preposition, the pronoun used is either **qui** or **lequel**. In English, the relative pronoun is seldom used and the preposition is frequently placed after the verb or at the end of the sentence.

qui is generally used after a preposition when referring to people:

où est la fille *avec* qui je dansais ?
where's the girl I was dancing *with*?

montre-moi la personne *à* qui tu as vendu ton vélo
show me the person you sold your bike *to*

lequel is often used after a preposition when referring to things:

l'immeuble *dans* lequel j'habite est très moderne
the building (which) I live *in* is very modern

je ne reconnais pas la voiture *avec* laquelle il est venu
I don't recognize the car (which) he came *in*

lequel is also used when referring to persons after the prepositions **entre** (between) and **parmi** (among):

des touristes, *parmi* lesquels il y avait des Japonais
tourists, among whom were (some) Japanese people

il aimait deux filles, *entre* lesquelles il hésitait
he loved two girls, between whom he was torn

e) *DONT*

dont (of which, of whom, whose) is frequently used instead of **de qui**, **duquel** etc. It means:

i) *of which, of whom:*

un métier *dont* il est fier
a job (which) he is proud of

Care must be taken with verbs that are normally followed by **de** + object: **de** is not always translated by 'of' in English, and is sometimes not translated at all (see section on verb constructions p 193-4):

voilà les choses *dont* j'ai besoin
here are the things (*which*) I need

les gens *dont* tu parles ne m'intéressent pas
I'm not interested in the people you're talking about

l'enfant *dont* elle s'occupe n'est pas le sien
the child she is looking *after* is not hers

ii) *whose*

dont is also used to translate the English pronoun 'whose'. In French, the construction of the clause that follows **dont** differs from English in two ways:

★ the noun which follows **dont** is used with the definite article (**le, la, les, l'**):

mon copain, *dont le* père a eu un accident
my friend, whose father had an accident

★ the word order in French is **dont** + subject + verb + object:

je te présente Hélène, *dont* tu connais déjà le frère
this is Helen, whose brother you already know

c'était dans une petite rue *dont* j'ai oublié le nom
it was in a small street the name of which I've forgotten

Note: **dont** cannot be used after a preposition:

une jolie maison, *près* de laquelle il y a un petit lac
a pretty house, *next* to which there is a small lake

OU

i) **où** generally means 'where':

l'hôtel où on a logé était très confortable
the hotel where we stayed was very comfortable

ii) **où** often replaces a preposition + **lequel**, meaning 'in/to/on/at which' etc:

c'est la maison où je suis né
that's the house in which/where I was born

une surprise-partie où il a invité tous ses amis
a party to which he invited all his friends

iii) **où** is also used to translate 'when' after a noun referring to time:

le jour où	**la fois où**	**le moment où**
the day when	the time when	the moment when

tu te rappelles le soir où on a raté le dernier métro ?
do you remember the evening when we missed the last train?

g) CE QUI, CE QUE

ce is used before **qui** and **que** when the relative pronoun does not refer to a specific noun. Both **ce qui** and **ce que** mean 'that which', 'the thing which', and are usually translated by 'what':

i) **ce qui**

ce qui is followed by a verb without a subject (**qui** is the subject):

ce qui s'est passé ne vous regarde pas
what happened is none of your business

ce qui m'étonne, c'est sa patience
what surprises me is his patience

Note the comma and the **c'**

ii) **ce que**

ce que (**ce qu'** before a vowel or a silent **h**) is followed by a verb with its own subject (**que** is the object):

fais ce que tu veux	**c'est ce qu'il a dit ?**
do what you want	is that what he said?

ce que vous me demandez est impossible
what you're asking me is impossible

iii) **tout ce qui/que**

tout is used in front of **ce qui/que** in the sense of 'all that', 'everything that':

> **c'est tout ce que je veux**   **tout ce que tu as fait**
> that's all I want   everything you did

> **tu n'as pas eu de mal ; c'est tout ce qui compte**
> you weren't hurt; that's all that matters

iv) **ce qui/que** are often used in indirect questions (see p 69):

> **je ne sais pas ce qu'ils vont dire**
> I don't know what they'll say

v) when referring to a previous clause, **ce qui** and **ce que** are translated by 'which':

> **elle est en retard, ce qui arrive souvent**
> she's late, which happens often

vi) **ce que/qui** are used with a preposition (when the preposition refers to **ce**):

> **ce n'est pas étonnant, après ce qui lui est arrivé**
> it's not surprising, after what happened to him

> **il y a du vrai dans ce que vous dites**
> there is some truth in what you say

But: **QUOI** is used instead of **ce que** after a preposition when the preposition refers to **que**, and not to **ce**:

> **c'est ce à quoi je pensais**
> that's what I was thinking about

vii) **ce que** is used with the preposition **de** when **de** refers to **ce**:

> **je suis fier de ce qu'il a fait**
> I'm proud of what he did

But: **ce dont** is used instead of **de + ce que** when **de** refers to **que**, and not to **ce**:

> **c'est ce dont j'avais peur**
> that's what I was afraid of

> **tu as trouvé ce dont tu avais besoin ?**
> did you find what you needed?

7. VERBS

A.   REGULAR CONJUGATIONS

1.   Conjugations

There are three main conjugations in French, which are determined
by the infinitive endings. The first conjugation verbs, by far the largest
category, end in **-er** (eg aimer) and will be referred to as **-er** verbs; the
second conjugation verbs end in **-ir** (eg finir) and will be referred to as
-ir verbs; the third conjugation verbs, the smallest category, end in **-re**
(eg vendre) and will be referred to as **-re** verbs.

2.   Simple tenses

The simple tenses in French are:

   a) present
   b) imperfect
   c) future
   d) conditional
   e) past historic
   f) present subjunctive
   g) imperfect subjunctive

For the use of the different tenses, see p 117-35.

3. Formation of tenses

The tenses are formed by adding the following endings to the stem of the verb (mainly the stem of the infinitive) as set out in the following section:

a) *PRESENT:* stem of the infinitive + the following endings:

-er VERBS	-ir VERBS	-re VERBS
-e, -es, -e,	-is, -is, -it,	-s, -s, -,
-ons, -ez, -ent	-issons, -issez, -issent	-ons, -ez, -ent

AIMER	FINIR	VENDRE
j'aime	je finis	je vends
tu aimes	tu finis	tu vends
il aime	il finit	il vend
elle aime	elle finit	elle vend
nous aimons	nous finissons	nous vendons
vous aimez	vous finissez	vous vendez
ils aiment	ils finissent	ils vendent
elles aiment	elles finissent	elles vendent

b) *IMPERFECT:* stem of the first person plural of the present tense (ie the '**nous**' form minus **-ons**) + the following endings:

-ais, -ais, -ait, -ions, -iez, -aient

j'aimais	je finissais	je vendais
tu aimais	tu finissais	tu vendais
il aimait	il finissait	il vendait
elle aimait	elle finissait	elle vendait
nous aimions	nous finissions	nous vendions
vous aimiez	vous finissiez	vous vendiez
ils aimaient	ils finissaient	ils vendaient
elles aimaient	elles finissaient	elles vendaient

Note: the only irregular imperfect is **être**: **j'étais** etc.

c) *FUTURE:* infinitive + the following endings:

-ai, -as, -a, -ons, -ez, -ont

Note: Verbs ending in -re drop the final e of the infinitive

j'aimerai	je finirai	je vendrai
tu aimeras	tu finiras	tu vendras
il aimera	il finira	il vendra
elle aimera	elle finira	elle vendra
nous aimerons	nous finirons	nous vendrons
vous aimerez	vous finirez	vous vendrez
ils aimeront	ils finiront	ils vendront
elles aimeront	elles finiront	elles vendront

d) *CONDITIONAL:* infinitive + the following endings:

-ais, -ais, -ait, -ions, -iez, -aient

Note: Verbs ending in -re drop the final e of the infinitive

j'aimerais	je finirais	je vendrais
tu aimerais	tu finirais	tu vendrais
il aimerait	il finirait	il vendrait
elle aimerait	elle finirait	elle vendrait
nous aimerions	nous finirions	nous vendrions
vous aimeriez	vous finiriez	vous vendriez
ils aimeraient	ils finiraient	ils vendraient
elles aimeraient	elles finiraient	elles vendraient

e) *PAST HISTORIC:* stem of the infinitive + the following endings:

-er VERBS	-ir VERBS	-re VERBS
-ai, -as, -a, -âmes, -âtes, -èrent	-is, -is, -it, -îmes, -îtes, -irent	-is, -is, -it, -îmes, -îtes, -irent
j'aimai	je finis	je vendis
tu aimas	tu finis	tu vendis
il aima	il finit	il vendit
elle aima	elle finit	elle vendit
nous aimâmes	nous finîmes	nous vendîmes
vous aimâtes	vous finîtes	vous vendîtes
ils aimèrent	ils finirent	ils vendirent
elles aimèrent	elles finirent	elles vendirent

f) *PRESENT SUBJUNCTIVE:* stem of the first person plural of the present indicative + the following endings:

-e, -es, -e, -ions, -iez, -ent

j'aime	je finisse	je vende
tu aimes	tu finisses	tu vendes
il aime	il finisse	il vende
elle aime	elle finisse	elle vende
nous aimions	nous finissions	nous vendions
vous aimiez	vous finissiez	vous vendiez
ils aiment	ils finissent	ils vendent
elles aiment	elles finissent	elles vendent

g) *IMPERFECT SUBJUNCTIVE:* stem of the first person singular of the past historic + the following endings:

-er VERBS	-ir VERBS	-re VERBS
-asse, -asses, -ât,	**-isse, -isses, -ît,**	**-isse, -isses, -ît,**
-assions, -assiez,	**-issions, -issiez,**	**-issions, -issiez,**
-assent	**-issent**	**-issent**
j'aimasse	je finisse	je vendisse
tu aimasses	tu finisses	tu vendisses
il aimât	il finît	il vendît
elle aimât	elle finît	elle vendît
nous aimassions	nous finissions	nous vendissions
vous aimassiez	vous finissiez	vous vendissiez
ils aimassent	ils finissent	ils vendissent
elles aimassent	elles finissent	elles vendissent

B. STANDARD SPELLING IRREGULARITIES

Spelling irregularities only affect -er verbs.

1. Verbs ending in -cer and -ger

a) Verbs ending in **-cer** require a cedilla under the **c** (**ç**) before an **a** or an **o** to preserve the soft sound of the **c**: eg **commencer** (to begin).

b) Verbs ending in **-ger** require an **-e** after the **g** before an **a** or an **o** to preserve the soft sound of the **g**: eg **manger** (to eat).

Changes to **-cer** and **-ger** verbs occur in the following tenses: present, imperfect, past historic, imperfect subjunctive and present participle.

COMMENCER	MANGER

PRESENT

je commence	je mange
tu commences	tu manges
il commence	il mange
elle commence	elle mange
nous **commençons**	nous **mangeons**
vous commencez	vous mangez
ils commencent	ils mangent
elles commencent	elles mangent

IMPERFECT

je **commençais**	je **mangeais**
tu **commençais**	tu **mangeais**
il **commençait**	il **mangeait**
elle **commençait**	elle **mangeait**
nous commencions	nous mangions
vous commenciez	vous mangiez
ils **commençaient**	ils **mangeaient**
elles **commençaient**	elles **mangeaient**

PAST HISTORIC

je **commençai**	je **mangeai**
tu **commenças**	tu **mangeas**
il **commença**	il **mangea**
elle **commença**	elle **mangea**
nous **commençâmes**	nous **mangeâmes**
vous **commençâtes**	vous **mangeâtes**
ils commencèrent	ils mangèrent
elles commencèrent	elles mangèrent

IMPERFECT SUBJUNCTIVE

je **commençassse**	je **mangeasse**
tu **commençasses**	tu **mangeasses**
il **commençât**	il **mangeât**
elle **commençât**	elle **mangeât**
nous **commençassions**	nous **mangeassions**
vous **commençassiez**	vous **mangeassiez**
ils **commençassent**	ils **mangeassent**
elles **commençassent**	elles **mangeassent**

PRESENT PARTICIPLE

commençant   **mangeant**

2. Verbs ending in -*eler* and -*eter*

a) Verbs ending in -**eler**

Verbs ending in -**eler** double the **l** before a silent **e** (ie before -**e**, -**es**, -**ent** of the present indicative and subjunctive, and throughout the future and conditional): eg **appeler** (to call).

PRESENT INDICATIVE	PRESENT SUBJUNCTIVE
j'**appelle**	j'**appelle**
tu **appelles**	tu **appelles**
il **appelle**	il **appelle**
elle **appelle**	elle **appelle**
nous appelons	nous appelions
vous appelez	vous appeliez
ils **appellent**	ils **appellent**
elles **appellent**	elles **appellent**

FUTURE	CONDITIONAL
j'**appellerai**	j'**appellerais**
tu **appelleras**	tu **appellerais**
il **appellera**	il **appellerait**
elle **appellera**	elle **appellerait**
nous **appellerons**	nous **appellerions**
vous **appellerez**	vous **appelleriez**
ils **appelleront**	ils **appelleraient**
elles **appelleront**	elles **appelleraient**

But: some verbs in -**eler** including the following are conjugated like **acheter** (see p 100):

celer	to conceal
congeler	to (deep-)freeze
déceler	to detect, reveal
dégeler	to defrost
geler	to freeze
harceler	to harass
marteler	to hammer
modeler	to model
peler	to peel

b) Verbs ending in **-eter**

Verbs ending in **-eter** double the **t** before a silent **e** (ie before **-e, -es, -ent** of the present indicative and subjunctive, and throughout the future and conditional): eg **jeter** (to throw).

PRESENT INDICATIVE	PRESENT SUBJUNCTIVE
je **jette**	je **jette**
tu **jettes**	tu **jettes**
il **jette**	il **jette**
elle **jette**	elle **jette**
nous jetons	nous jetions
vous jetez	vous jetiez
ils **jettent**	ils **jettent**
elles **jettent**	elles **jettent**

FUTURE	CONDITIONAL
je **jetterai**	je **jetterais**
tu **jetteras**	tu **jetterais**
il **jettera**	il **jetterait**
elle **jettera**	elle **jetterait**
nous **jetterons**	nous **jetterions**
vous **jetterez**	vous **jetteriez**
ils **jetteront**	ils **jetteraient**
elles **jetterot**	elles **jetteraient**

But: some verbs in **-eter** including the following are conjugated like **acheter** (see p 100):

crocheter	to pick (*lock*)
fureter	to ferret about
haleter	to pant
racheter	to buy back

c) Verbs ending in **-oyer** and **-uyer**

In verbs ending in **-oyer** and **-uyer** the y changes to i before a silent e
(ie before **-e, -es, -ent** of the present indicative and subjunctive, and
throughout the future and conditional): eg **employer** (to use) and
ennuyer (to bore).

PRESENT INDICATIVE	PRESENT SUBJUNCTIVE
j'**emploie**	j'**emploie**
tu **emploies**	tu **emploies**
il **emploie**	il **emploie**
elle **emploie**	elle **emploie**
nous employons	nous employions
vous employez	vous employiez
ils **emploient**	ils **emploient**
elles **emploient**	elles **emploient**

FUTURE	CONDITIONAL
j'**emploierai**	j'**emploierais**
tu **emploieras**	tu **emploierais**
il **emploiera**	il **emploierait**
elle **emploiera**	elle **emploierait**
nous **emploierons**	nous **emploierions**
vous **emploierez**	vous **emploieriez**
ils **emploieront**	ils **emploieraient**
elles **emploieront**	elles **emploieraient**

Note: **envoyer** (to send) and **renvoyer** (to dismiss) have an irregular future
and conditional: **j'enverrai, j'enverrais; je renverrai, je
renverrais**.

d) Verbs ending in **-ayer**

In verbs ending in **-ayer**, eg **balayer** (to sweep), **payer** (to pay),
essayer (to try), the change from y to i is optional:

eg je **balaie**	*or*	je **balaye**
je **paie**	*or*	je **paye**
j'**essaie**	*or*	j'**essaye**

e) Verbs in **e** + consonant + **er**

Verbs like **acheter**, **enlever**, **mener**, **peser** change the (last) **e** of the stem to **è** before a silent **e** (ie before **-e**, **-es**, **-ent** of the present indicative and subjunctive and throughout the future and conditional):

PRESENT INDICATIVE	*PRESENT SUBJUNCTIVE*
j'**achète**	j'**achète**
tu **achètes**	tu **achètes**
il **achète**	il **achète**
elle **achète**	elle **achète**
nous achetons	nous achetions
vous achetez	vous achetiez
ils **achètent**	ils **achètent**
elles **achètent**	elles **achètent**

FUTURE	*CONDITIONAL*
j'**achèterai**	j'**achèterais**
tu **achèteras**	tu **achèterais**
il **achètera**	il **achèterait**
elle **achètera**	elle **achèterait**
nous **achèterons**	nous **achèterions**
vous **achèterez**	vous **achèteriez**
ils **achèteront**	ils **achèteraient**
elles **achèteront**	elles **achèteraient**

Verbs conjugated like **acheter** include:

achever to complete	**haleter** to pant
amener to bring	**harceler** to harass
celer to conceal	**lever** to lift
crever to burst	**marteler** to hammer
crocheter to pick (*lock*)	**mener** to lead
élever to raise	**modeler** to model
emmener to take away	**peler** to peel
enlever to remove	**peser** to weigh
étiqueter to label	**se promener** to go for a walk
fureter to ferret about	**semer** to sow
geler to freeze	**soulever** to lift

f) Verbs in **é** + consonant + **er**

Verbs like **espérer** (to hope) change **é** to **è** before a silent **e** in the present indicative and subjunctive. BUT in the future and conditional **é** is retained.

PRESENT INDICATIVE	*PRESENT SUBJUNCTIVE*
j'**espère**	j'**espère**
tu **espères**	tu **espères**
il **espère**	il **espère**
elle **espère**	elle **espère**
nous espérons	nous espérions
vous espérez	vous espériez
ils **espèrent**	ils **espèrent**
elles **espèrent**	elles **espèrent**

FUTURE	*CONDITIONAL*
j'**espérerai**	j'**espérerais**
tu **espéreras**	tu **espérerais**
il **espérera**	il **espérerait**
elle **espérera**	elle **espérerait**
nous **espérerons**	nous **espérerions**
vous **espérerez**	vous **espéreriez**
ils **espéreront**	ils **espéreraient**
elles **espéreront**	elles **espéreraient**

Verbs conjugated like **espérer** include verbs in **-éder, -érer, -éter** etc:

accéder	to accede to
céder	to yield
célébrer	to celebrate
compléter	to complete
considérer	to consider
décéder	to die
digérer	to digest
gérer	to manage
inquiéter	to worry
libérer	to free
opérer	to operate
pénétrer	to penetrate

persévérer	to persevere
posséder	to possess
précéder	to precede
préférer	to prefer
protéger	to protect
récupérer	to recover
refréner	to curb
régler	to rule
régner	to reign
répéter	to repeat, to rehearse
révéler	to reveal
sécher	to dry
succéder	to succeed
suggérer	to suggest
tolérer	to tolerate

C. AUXILIARIES AND THE FORMATION OF COMPOUND TENSES

1. Formation

a) The two auxiliary verbs **AVOIR** and **ETRE** are used with the past participle of a verb to form compound tenses.

b) *The past participle*

The regular past participle is formed by taking the stem of the infinitive and adding the following endings:

-er	-ir	-re
aim(**er**) + **é**	fin(**ir**) + **i**	vend(**re**) + **u**
aimé	fini	vend**u**

For the agreement of past participles see p 147-9.

c) *Compound tenses*

In French there are seven compound tenses: perfect, pluperfect, future perfect, past conditional (conditional perfect), past anterior, perfect subjunctive, pluperfect subjunctive.

2. Verbs conjugated with AVOIR

a) *PERFECT*	b) *PLUPERFECT*
present of **avoir** + past participle	imperfect of **avoir** + past participle
j'ai aimé	j'avais aimé
tu as aimé	tu avais aimé
il a aimé	il avait aimé
elle a aimé	elle avait aimé
nous avons aimé	nous avions aimé
vous avez aimé	vous aviez aimé
ils ont aimé	ils avaient aimé
elles ont aimé	elles avaient aimé

c) *FUTURE PERFECT*

future of **avoir** +
past participle

j' aurai aimé
tu auras aimé
il aura aimé
elle aura aimé
nous aurons aimé
vous aurez aimé
ils auront aimé
elles auront aimé

d) *PAST CONDITIONAL*

conditional of **avoir** +
past participle

j' aurais aimé
tu aurais aimé
il aurait aimé
elle aurait aimé
nous aurions aimé
vous auriez aimé
ils auraient aimé
elles auraient aimé

e) *PAST ANTERIOR*

past historic of **avoir** +
past participle

j' eus aimé
tu eus aimé
il eut aimé
elle eut aimé
nous eûmes aimé
vous eûtes aimé
ils eurent aimé
elles eurent aimé

f) *PERFECT SUBJUNCTIVE*

present subjunctive of
avoir + past participle

j'aie aimé
tu aies aimé
il ait aimé
elle ait aimé
nous ayons aimé
vous ayez aimé
ils aient aimé
elles aient aimé

g) *PLUPERFECT SUBJUNCTIVE*

pluperfect subjunctive of
avoir + past participle

j'eusse aimé
tu eusses aimé
il eût aimé
elle eût aimé
nous eussions aimé
vous eussiez aimé
ils eussent aimé
elles eussent aimé

3. Verbs conjugated with ETRE

a) PERFECT

present of **être** +
past participle

je suis arrivé(e)
tu es arrivé(e)
il est arrivé
elle est arrivée
nous sommes arrivé(e)s
vous êtes arrivé(e)(s)
ils sont arrivés
elles sont arrivées

b) PLUPERFECT

imperfect of **être** +
past participle

j'étais arrivé(e)
tu étais arrivé(e)
il était arrivé
elle était arrivée
nous étions arrivé(e)s
vous étiez arrivé(e)(s)
ils étaient arrivés
elles étaient arrivées

c) FUTURE PERFECT

future of **être** +
past participle

je serai arrivé(e)
tu seras arrivé(e)
il sera arrivé
elle sera arrivée
nous serons arrivé(e)s
vous serez arrivé(e)(s)
ils seront arrivés
elles seront arrivées

d) PAST CONDITIONAL

conditional of **être** +
past participle

je serais arrivé(e)
tu serais arrivé(e)
il serait arrivé
elle serait arrivée
nous serions arrivé(e)s
vous seriez arrivé(e)(s)
ils seraient arrivés
elles seraient arrivées

e) PAST ANTERIOR

past historic of **être** +
past participle

je fus arrivé(e)
tu fus arrivé(e)
il fut arrivé
elle fut arrivée
nous fûmes arrivé(e)s
vous fûtes arrivé(e)(s)
ils furent arrivés
elles furent arrivées

f) *PERFECT SUBJUNCTIVE* g) *PLUPERFECT SUBJUNCTIVE*

present subjunctive of **être** + past participle

imperfect subjunctive of **être** + past participle

je sois arrivé(e)	**je fusse arrivé(e)**
tu sois arrivé(e)	**tu fusses arrivé(e)**
il soit arrivé	**il fût arrivé**
elle soit arrivée	**elle fût arrivée**
nous soyons arrivé(e)s	**nous fussions arrivé(e)s**
vous soyez arrivé(e)(s)	**vous fussiez arrivé(e)(s)**
ils soient arrivés	**ils fussent arrivés**
elles soient arrivées	**elles fussent arrivées**

4. AVOIR or ETRE?

a) *Verbs conjugated with **avoir***

The compound tenses of most verbs are formed with **avoir**:

j'ai marqué un but　　**elle a dansé toute la nuit**
I scored a goal　　she danced all night

b) *Verbs conjugated with **être***

i) all reflexive verbs (see p 110):

je me suis baigné
I had a bath

ii) the following verbs (mainly of motion):

aller	to go
arriver	to arrive
descendre	to go/come down
entrer	to go/come in
monter	to go/come up
mourir	to die
naître	to be born
partir	to leave
passer	to go through, to drop in
rester	to remain
retourner	to return
sortir	to go/come out
tomber	to fall
venir	to come

and most of their compounds:

revenir	to come back
devenir	to become
parvenir	to reach, to manage to
rentrer	to return home
remonter	to go up again
redescendre	to go down again

But: **prévenir** (to warn) and **subvenir** (to provide for) take a direct object and are conjugated with **avoir**.

Note: **passer** can also be conjugated with **avoir**:

il a passé par Paris
he went via Paris

Some of the verbs listed above can take a direct object. In such cases they are conjugated with **avoir** and can take on a different meaning:

descendre	to take/bring down, to go down (*the stairs, a slope*)
monter	to take/bring up, to go up (*the stairs, a slope*)
rentrer	to take/bring/put in
retourner	to turn over
sortir	to take/bring out

les élèves sont sortis à midi
the pupils came out at midday

les élèves ont sorti leurs livres
the pupils took out their books

elle n'est pas encore descendue
she hasn't come down yet

elle a descendu un vieux tableau de l'atelier
she brought an old painting down from the loft

elle a descendu l'escalier
she came down the stairs

les prisonniers sont montés sur le toit
the prisoners climbed on to the roof

le garçon a monté les bouteilles de vin de la cave
the waiter brought the bottles of wine up from the cellar

nous sommes rentrés tard
we returned home late

j'ai rentré la voiture dans le garage
I put the car in the garage

je serais retourné à Paris
I would have returned to Paris

le jardinier a retourné le sol
the gardener turned over the soil

ils sont sortis de la piscine
they got out of the swimming pool

le gangster a sorti un revolver
the gangster pulled out a revolver

D. REFLEXIVE VERBS

1. Definition

Reflexive verbs are so called because they 'reflect' the action back onto the subject. Reflexive verbs are always accompanied by a reflexive pronoun; eg in the following sentence:

I looked at myself in the mirror

'myself' is the reflexive pronoun.

je lave la voiture	**je *me* lave**
I'm washing the car	I'm washing *myself*
j'ai couché le bébé	**je *me* suis couché**
I put the baby to bed	I went to bed (I put *myself* to bed)

2. Reflexive pronouns

They are:

PERSON	SINGULAR	PLURAL
1st	**me (m')**	**nous**
	myself	ourselves
2nd	**te (t')**	**vous**
	yourself	yourself/selves
3rd	**se (s')**	**se (s')**
	himself, herself, itself, oneself	themselves

Note:

a) **m', t'** and **s'** are used instead of **me, te** and **se** in front of a vowel or a silent **h**:

   tu t'amuses ? — non, je m'ennuie
   are you enjoying yourself? — no, I'm bored

   il s'habille à la salle de bain
   he gets dressed in the bathroom

b) French reflexive pronouns are often not translated in English:

je me demande si ...	**ils se moquent de moi**
I wonder if ...	they're making fun of me

c) Plural reflexive pronouns can also be used to express reciprocal actions; in this case they are translated by 'each other' or 'one another':

nous nous détestons	**ils ne se parlent pas**
we hate one another	they're not talking to each other

d) **se** can mean 'ourselves' or 'each other' when it is used with the pronoun **on** meaning 'we' (see p 64):

on s'est perdu	**on se connaît**
we got lost	we know each other

3. Position of reflexive pronouns

Reflexive pronouns are placed immediately before the verb, except in positive commands, where they follow the verb and are linked to it by a hyphen:

tu te dépêches ?	**dépêchons-nous !**
will you hurry up?	let's hurry!
ne t'inquiète pas	**ne vous fiez pas à lui**
don't worry	don't trust him

Note: reflexive pronouns change to emphatic (disjunctive) pronouns in positive commands:

elle doit se reposer	**repose-toi**
she needs to rest	have a rest

4. Conjugation of reflexive verbs

a) *Simple tenses*

These are formed in the same way as for non-reflexive verbs, except that a reflexive pronoun is used.

b) *Compound tenses*

These are formed with the auxiliary **être** followed by the past participle of the verb.

A full conjugation table is given on p 176.

5. Agreement of the past participle

a) In most cases, the reflexive pronoun is a direct object and the past participle of the verb agrees in number and in gender with the reflexive pronoun:

il s'est trompé	**elle s'est endormie**
he made a mistake	she fell asleep
ils se sont excusés	**elles se sont assises**
they apologised	they sat down

b) When the reflexive pronoun is used as an indirect object, the past participle does not change:

nous nous sommes écrit	**elle se l'est acheté**
we wrote to each other	she bought it for herself

When the reflexive verb has a direct object, the reflexive pronoun is the indirect object of the reflexive verb and the past participle does not agree with it:

Caroline s'est tordu la cheville
Caroline sprained her ankle

vous vous êtes lavé les mains, les filles ?
did you wash your hands, girls?

6. Common reflexive verbs

s'en aller	**s'éloigner (de)**	**se moquer de**
to go away	to move away (from)	to laugh at
s'amuser	**s'endormir**	**s'occuper de**
to have fun	to fall asleep	to take care of
s'appeler	**s'ennuyer**	**se passer**
to be called	to be bored	to happen
s'approcher (de)	**s'étonner (de)**	**se passer de**
to come near	to be surprised (at)	to do without
s'arrêter	**s'excuser (de)**	**se promener**
to stop	to apologize (for)	to go for a walk
s'asseoir	**se fâcher**	**se rappeler**
to sit down	to get angry/fall out	to remember

s'attendre à
to expect

se baigner
to have a bath

se battre
to fight

se blesser
to hurt oneself

se coucher
to go to bed

se débarrasser de
to get rid of

se demander
to wonder

se dépêcher
to hurry

se déshabiller
to undress

se diriger vers
to move towards

s'écrier
to cry out/exclaim

s'habiller
to get dressed

se hâter
to hurry

s'inquiéter
to worry

s'installer
to settle down

se laver
to wash

se lever
to get up

se mêler de
to meddle with

se mettre à
to start

se mettre en route
to set off

se raser
to shave

se renseigner
to make enquiries

se ressembler
to look alike

se retourner
to turn round

se réveiller
to wake up

se sauver
to run away

se souvenir (de)
to remember

se taire
to be/keep quiet

se tromper
to be mistaken

se trouver
to be (situated)

E. IMPERSONAL VERBS

1. Conjugation

Impersonal verbs are used only in the third person singular and in the infinitive. The subject is always the impersonal pronoun **il** = it.

il neige it's snowing	**il y a du brouillard** it's foggy

2. List of impersonal verbs

a) *verbs describing the weather:*

i) **faire** + adjective:

il fait beau/chaud it's fine/warm	**il fait frais/froid** it's cool/cold
il fera beau demain the weather will be good tomorrow	**il va faire très froid** it will be very cold

ii) **faire** + noun:

il fait beau temps the weather is nice	**il fait mauvais temps** the weather is bad

Note:

il fait jour it's day(light)	**il fait nuit** it's dark

iii) other impersonal verbs and verbs used impersonally to describe the weather:

il gèle	**(geler)**	it's freezing
il grêle	**(grêler)**	it's hailing
il neige	**(neiger)**	it's snowing
il pleut	**(pleuvoir)**	it's raining
il tonne	**(tonner)**	it's thundering

Note: some of these verbs may be used personally:

je gèle	I am freezing

iv) **il y a** + noun:

il y a des nuages	it's cloudy
il y a du brouillard	it's foggy
il y a du verglas	it's icy

b) *être*

   i) **il est** + noun:

il est cinq heures	it's five o'clock
il était une fois un géant	there was once a giant

   ii) **il est** + adjective + **de** + infinitive:

il est difficile de	it's difficult to
il est facile de	it's easy to
il est nécessaire de	it's necessary to
il est inutile de	it's useless to
il est possible de	it's possible to

   il est difficile d'en parler
   it is difficult to speak about it

Note: the indirect object pronoun in French corresponds to the English 'for me, for him' etc:

   il m'est difficile d'en parler
   it is difficult for me to speak about it

   iii) **il est** + adjective + **que**:

il est douteux que	it's doubtful that
il est évident que	it's clear that
il est possible que	it's possible that
il est probable que	it's probable that
il est peu probable que	it's unlikely that
il est vrai que	it's true that

Note: **que** may be followed by the indicative or the subjunctive (see p 126):

   il est probable qu'il ne viendra pas
   he probably won't come

   il est peu probable qu'il vienne
   it's unlikely that he'll come

c) *arriver, se passer (to happen)*

il est arrivé une chose curieuse	**que se passe-t-il ?**
a strange thing happened	what's happening?

d) *exister (to exist), rester (to remain), manquer (to be missing)*

> **il existe trois exemplaires de ce livre**
> there are three copies of this book

> **il me restait six francs**   **il me manque vingt francs**
> I had six francs left   I am twenty francs short

e) *paraître, sembler (to seem)*

> **il paraîtrait/semblerait qu'il ait changé d'avis**
> it would appear that he has changed his mind

> **il paraît qu'il va se marier**
> it seems he's going to get married

> **il me semble que le professeur s'est trompé**
> it seems to me that the teacher has made a mistake

f) *other common impersonal verbs*

i) **s'agir** (to be a matter of):

may be followed by a noun, a pronoun or an infinitive:

> **il s'agit de ton avenir**   **de quoi s'agit-il ?**
> it's about your future   what is it about?

> **il s'agit de trouver le coupable**
> we must find the culprit

ii) **falloir** (to be necessary):

may be followed by a noun, an infinitive or the subjunctive:

> **il faut deux heures pour aller à Paris**
> it takes two hours to get to Paris

> **il me faut plus de temps**
> I need more time

> **il faudra rentrer plus tôt ce soir**
> we'll have to come home earlier tonight

> **il faut que tu parles à Papa**
> you'll have to speak to your Dad

iii) **suffire** (to be enough):

may be followed by a noun, an infinitive or the subjunctive:

> **il suffit de peu de chose pour être heureux**
> it takes little to be happy

> **il suffit de passer le pont**
> you only have to cross the bridge

> **il suffira qu'ils te donnent le numéro de téléphone**
> they will only have to give you the telephone number

iv) **valoir mieux** (to be better):

may be followed by an infinitive or the subjunctive:

> **il vaudrait mieux prendre le car**
> it would be better to take the coach

> **il vaut mieux que vous ne sortiez pas seule le soir**
> you'd better not go out alone at night

F. TENSES

For the formation of the different tenses, see p 92-4 and 103-6.

Note: French has no continuous tenses (as in 'I am eating', 'I was going', 'I will be arriving'). The 'be' and '-ing' parts of English continuous tenses are not translated as separate words. Instead, the equivalent tense is used in French:

ENGLISH	FRENCH
I am eating	**je mange**
I will be eating	**je mangerai**

1. PRESENT

The present is used to describe what someone does/something that happens regularly, or what someone is doing/something that is happening at the time of speaking.

a) *regular actions*

il travaille dans un bureau
he works in an office

je lis rarement le journal
I seldom read the paper

b) *continuous actions*

ne le dérangez pas, il travaille
don't disturb him, he's working

je ne peux pas venir, je garde mon petit frère
I can't come, I'm looking after my little brother

Note: the continuous nature of the action can also be expressed by using the phrase **être en train de** (to be in the process of) + infinitive:

je suis en train de cuisiner
I'm (busy) cooking

c) *immediate future*

je pars demain
I'm leaving tomorrow

But: the present cannot be used after **quand** and other conjunctions of
time when the future is implied (see p 124):

>**je le ferai quand j'aurai le temps**
>I'll do it when I have the time

d) *general truths*

>**la vie est dure**
>life is hard

2. IMPERFECT

The imperfect is a past tense used to express what someone was doing
or what someone used to do or to describe something in the past. The
imperfect refers particularly to something that *continued* over a
period of time, as opposed to something that happened at a specific
point in time.

a) *continuous actions*

the imperfect describes an action that was happening eg when
something else took place (imperfect means unfinished):

>**il prenait un bain quand le téléphone a sonné**
>he was having a bath when the phone rang

>**excuse-moi, je pensais à autre chose**
>I'm sorry, I was thinking of something else

Note: the continuous nature of the action can be emphasised by using **être
en train de** + infinitive:

>**j'étais en train de faire le ménage**
>I was (busy) doing the housework

b) *regular actions in the past*

>**je le voyais souvent quand il habitait dans le quartier**
>I used to see him often when he lived in this area

>**quand il était plus jeune il voyageait beaucoup**
>when he was younger he used to travel a lot

c) *description in the past*

>**il faisait beau ce jour-là**
>the weather was fine that day

>**c'était formidable !**
>it was great!

>**elle portait une robe bleue**
>she wore a blue dress

>**elle donnait sur la rue**
>it looked onto the street

3. PERFECT

The perfect tense is a compound past tense, used to express *single* actions which have been completed, ie what someone did or what someone has done/has been doing or something that has happened or has been happening:

je l'ai envoyé lundi I sent it on Monday	**on est sorti hier soir** we went out last night
tu t'es bien amusé ? did you have a good time?	**je ne l'ai pas vu** I didn't see him
j'ai lu toute la journée I've been reading all day	**tu as déjà mangé ?** have you eaten?

Note: Perfect or imperfect?

In English, the simple past ('did', 'went', 'prepared') is used to describe both single and repeated actions in the past. In French, the perfect only describes single actions in the past, while repeated actions are expressed by the imperfect (they are sometimes signposted by 'used to'). Thus 'I went' should be translated 'j'allais' or 'je suis allé' depending on the nature of the action:

après dîner, je suis allé en ville
after dinner I went to town

l'an dernier, j'allais plus souvent au théâtre
last year, I went to the theatre more often

4. PAST HISTORIC

This tense is used in the same way as the perfect tense, to describe a single, completed action in the past (what someone did or something that happened). It is a literary tense, not common in everyday spoken French; it is found mainly as a narrative tense in written form:

le piéton ne vit pas arriver la voiture
the pedestrian didn't see the car coming

5. PLUPERFECT

This compound tense is used to express what someone had done/had been doing or something that had happened or had been happening:

il n'avait pas voulu aller avec eux
he hadn't wanted to go with them

elle était essoufflée parce qu'elle avait couru
she was out of breath because she'd been running

However, the pluperfect is not used as in English with **depuis** (for, since), or with **venir de** + infinitive (to have just done something). For details see p 123

il neigeait depuis une semaine
it had been snowing for a week

les pompiers venaient d'arriver
the firemen had just arrived

6. FUTURE

This tense is used to express what someone will do or will be doing or something that will happen or will be happening:

je ferai la vaisselle   **j'arriverai tard**
demain   I'll be arriving late
I'll do the dishes tomorrow

Note: the future and not the present as in English is used in time clauses introduced by **quand** (when) or other conjunctions of time where the future is implied (see p 124):

il viendra quand il le pourra
he'll come when he can

French makes frequent use of **aller** + infinitive (to be about to do something) to express the immediate future:

je vais vous expliquer ce qui s'est passé
I'll explain (to you) what happened

il va déménager la semaine prochaine
he's moving house next week

FUTURE PERFECT

This compound tense is used to describe what someone will have
done/will have been doing in the future or to describe something that
will have happened in the future:

j'aurai bientôt fini
I will soon have finished

In particular, it is used instead of the English perfect in time clauses
introduced by **quand** or other conjunctions of time where the future is
implied (see p 124):

appelle-moi quand tu auras fini
call me when you've finished

on rentrera dès qu'on aura fait les courses
we'll come back as soon as we've done our shopping

PAST ANTERIOR

This tense is used instead of the pluperfect to express an action that
preceded another action in the past (ie a past in the past). It is usually
introduced by a conjunction of time (translated by 'when', 'as soon as',
'after' etc) and the main verb is in the past historic:

il se coucha dès qu'ils furent partis
he went to bed as soon as they'd left

à peine eut-elle raccroché que le téléphone sonna
she'd hardly hung up when the telephone rang

Use of tenses with 'depuis' (for, since)

The present must be used instead of the perfect to describe actions
which started in the past and have continued until the present:

il habite ici depuis trois ans
he's been living here for three years

elle l'attend depuis ce matin
she's been waiting for him since this morning

but: The perfect, not the present, is used when the clause is negative or
when the action has been completed:

il n'a pas pris de vacances depuis longtemps
he hasn't taken any holidays for a long time

> **j'ai fini depuis un bon moment**
> I've been finished for quite a while

Note:

i) **il y a ... que** or **voilà ... que** are also used with the present tense to translate 'for':

> it's been ringing for ten minutes
> **ça sonne depuis dix minutes**
> **il y a dix minutes que ça sonne**
> **voilà dix minutes que ça sonne**

ii) **depuis que** is used when 'since' introduces a clause, ie when there is a verb following **depuis**:

> **elle dort depuis que vous êtes partis**
> she's been sleeping since you left

iii) do not confuse **depuis** (for, since) and **pendant** (for, during): **depuis** refers to the starting point of an action which is still going on and **pendant** refers to the duration of an action which is over and is used with the perfect:

> **il vit ici depuis deux mois**
> he's been living here for two months

> **il a vécu ici pendant deux mois**
> he lived here for two months

o) the imperfect must be used instead of the pluperfect to describe an action which had started in the past and was still going on at a given time:

> **elle le connaissait depuis son enfance**
> she had known him since her childhood

> **il attendait depuis trois heures quand on est arrivé**
> he had been waiting for three hours when we arrived

But: if the sentence is negative or if the action has been completed, the pluperfect and not the imperfect is used:

> **je n'étais pas allé au théâtre depuis des années**
> I hadn't been to the theatre for years

il était parti depuis peu
he'd been gone for a short while

note:

i) **il y avait ... que** + imperfect is also used to translate 'for':

she'd been living alone for a long time
elle habitait seule depuis longtemps
il y avait longtemps qu'elle habitait seule

ii) **depuis que** is used when 'since' introduces a clause; if it describes an action which was still going on at the time, it can be followed by the imperfect, otherwise it is followed by the pluperfect:

il pleuvait depuis que nous étions en vacances
it had been raining since we had been on holiday

il pleuvait depuis que nous étions arrivés
it had been raining since we arrived

iii) do not confuse **depuis** and **pendant**: **depuis** refers to the starting point of an action which is still going on and **pendant** refers to the duration of an action which is over; **pendant** is used with the pluperfect:

j'y travaillais depuis un an
I had been working there for a year

j'y avais travaillé pendant un an
I had worked there for a year

▶. Use of tenses with 'venir de'

venir de + infinitive means 'to have just done'.

if it describes something that has just happened, it is used in the present instead of the perfect:

l'avion vient d'arriver   **je viens de te le dire !**
the plane has just arrived   I've just told you!

if it describes something that had just happened, it is used in the imperfect instead of the pluperfect:

le film venait de   **je venais de rentrer**
commencer   I'd just got home
the film had just started

11. Use of tenses after conjunctions of time

quand	when
tant que	as long as
dès/aussitôt que	as soon as
lorsque	when
pendant que	while

Verbs which follow these conjunctions must be used in the following tenses:

a) *future instead of present:*

> **je te téléphonerai quand je serai prêt**
> I'll phone you when I am ready

> **on ira dès qu'il fera beau**
> we'll go as soon as the weather is fine

b) *future perfect instead of perfect* when the future is implied:

> **on rentrera dès qu'on aura fini les courses**
> we'll come back as soon as we've done our shopping

> **je t'appellerai dès qu'il sera arrivé**
> I'll call you as soon as he has arrived

c) *conditional present/perfect instead of perfect/pluperfect* in indirect speech:

> **il a dit qu'il sortirait quand il aurait fini**
> he said that he would come out when he had finished

For the tenses of the subjunctive and conditional, see p 125-9 and 131-2.

G. MOODS

1. THE SUBJUNCTIVE

In spoken everyday French, the only two subjunctive tenses that are used are the present and the perfect. The imperfect and the pluperfect subjunctive are found mainly in literature or in texts of a formal nature.

The subjunctive is always preceded by the conjunction **que** and is used in subordinate clauses when the subject of the subordinate clause is different from the subject of the main verb.

Some clauses introduced by **que** take the indicative. But the subjunctive must be used after the following:

a) *Verbs of emotion*

être content que	to be pleased that
être déçu que	to be disappointed that
être désolé que	to be sorry that
être étonné que	to be surprised that
être fâché que	to be annoyed that
être heureux que	to happy that
être surpris que	to be surprised that
être triste que	to be sad that
avoir peur que ... ne	to be afraid/to fear that
craindre que ... ne	to be afraid/to fear that
regretter que	to be sorry that

ils étaient contents que j'aille les voir
they were pleased (that) I went to visit them

je serais très étonné qu'il mente
I would be very surprised if he was lying

on regrette beaucoup que tu n'aies pas pu vendre ta voiture
we're very sorry (that) you couldn't sell your car

Note: ne is used after **craindre que** or **avoir peur que**, but does not have a negative meaning in itself and is not translated in English:

je crains que l'avion *ne* soit en retard
I'm afraid (that) the plane will be late

b) *Verbs of wishing and willing:*

aimer que	to like
désirer que	to wish (that)
préférer que	to prefer (that)
souhaiter que	to wish (that)
vouloir que	to want

Note: In English, such verbs are often used in the following type of construction: verb of willing + object + infinitive (eg I'd like you to listen); this type of construction is impossible in French, where a subjunctive clause has to be used:

je souhaite que tu réussisses
I hope you will succeed

il aimerait que je lui écrive plus souvent
he'd like me to write to him more often

voulez-vous que je vous y amène en voiture ?
would you like me to drive you there?

préférez-vous que je rappelle demain ?
would you rather I called back tomorrow?

c) *Impersonal constructions* (expressing necessity, possibility, doubt, denial, preference):

il faut que	it is necessary (that) (*must*)
il est nécessaire que	it is necessary that (*must*)
il est important que	it is important (that)
il est possible que	it is possible that (*may*)
il se peut que	it is possible that (*may*)
il est impossible que	it is impossible (that) (*can't*)
il est douteux que	it is doubtful whether
il est peu probable que	it is unlikely that
il semble que	it seems (that)
il est préférable que	it is preferable (that)
il vaut mieux que	it is better (that) (*had better*)
c'est dommage que	it is a pity (that)

Note: these expressions may be used in any appropriate tense:

il faut qu'on se dépêche
we must hurry

il était important que tu le saches
it was important that you should know

il se pourrait qu'elle change d'avis
she might change her mind

il est peu probable qu'ils s'y intéressent
they're unlikely to be interested in that

il semble qu'elle ait raison
she appears to be right

il vaudrait mieux que tu ne promettes rien
you'd better not promise anything

c'est dommage que vous vous soyez manqués
it's a pity you missed each other

d) *Some verbs and impersonal constructions expressing doubt or uncertainty* (mainly used negatively or interrogatively):

douter que	to doubt (that)
(ne pas) croire que	(not) to believe (that)
(ne pas) penser que	(not) to think (that)
(ne pas) être sûr que	(not) to be sure that
il n'est pas certain que	it isn't certain that
il n'est pas évident que	it isn't obvious that
il n'est pas sûr que	it isn't certain that
il n'est pas vrai que	it isn't true that

je doute fort qu'il veuille t'aider
I very much doubt whether he'll want to help you

croyez-vous qu'il y ait des places de libres ?
do you think there are any seats available?

on n'était pas sûr que ce soit le bon endroit
we weren't sure that it was the right place

il n'était pas certain qu'elle puisse gagner
it wasn't certain whether she could win

e) *attendre que* (to wait until, to wait for someone to do something):

> **attendons qu'il revienne**
> let's wait until he comes back

f) *Some subordinating conjunctions:*

bien que	although
quoique	although
sans que	without
pour que	so that
afin que	so that
à condition que	provided that
pourvu que	provided that
jusqu'à ce que	until
en attendant que	until
avant que ... (ne)	before
à moins que ... (ne)	unless
de peur que ... ne	for fear that
de crainte que ... ne	for fear that
de sorte que	so that
de façon que	so that
de manière que	so that

Note: When **ne** is shown in brackets, it may follow the conjunction, although it is seldom used in spoken French; it does not have a negative meaning, and is not translated in English.

> **il est allé travailler bien qu'il soit malade**
> he went to work although he was ill

> **elle est entrée sans que je la voie**
> she came in without me seeing her

> **voilà de l'argent pour que tu puisses aller au cinéma**
> here's some money so that you can go to the pictures

> **d'accord, pourvu que tu me promettes de ne pas le répéter**
> all right, as long as you promise not to tell anyone

> **tu l'as revu avant qu'il (ne) parte ?**
> did you see him again before he left?

> **je le ferai demain, à moins que ce (ne) soit urgent**
> I'll do it tomorrow, unless it's urgent

elle n'a pas fait de bruit de peur qu'il ne se réveille
she didn't make any noise, in case he would wake up

parle moins fort de sorte qu'elle ne nous entende pas
talk more quietly so that she doesn't hear us

Note: when **de façon/manière que** (so that) express a result, as
opposed to a purpose, the indicative is used instead of the
subjunctive:

il a fait du bruit, de sorte qu'elle l'*a entendu*
he made some noise, so that she heard him

g) *A superlative or adjectives like **premier** (first), **dernier** (last), **seul**
(only) followed by **qui** or **que**:*

c'était le coureur le plus rapide que j'aie jamais vu
he was the fastest runner I ever saw

But: the indicative is used with a statement of fact rather than the
expression of an opinion:

c'est le coureur le plus rapide qui a gagné
it was the fastest runner who won

h) *Negative and indefinite pronouns (eg **rien**, **personne**,
quelqu'un) followed by **qui** or **que**:*

je ne connais personne qui sache aussi bien chanter
I don't know anyone who can sing so well

il n'y a aucune chance qu'il réussisse
he hasn't got a chance of succeeding

ils cherchent quelqu'un qui puisse garder le bébé
they're looking for someone who can look after the baby

2. Avoiding the subjunctive

The subjunctive can be avoided, as is the tendency with modern
spoken French, provided that both verbs in the sentence have the same
subject. It is replaced by an infinitive introduced by the preposition
de, the preposition **à** or by no preposition at all (see p 136-40).

a) *de* + *infinitive replaces the subjunctive after:*

i) verbs of emotion:

j'ai été étonné d'apprendre la nouvelle
I was surprised to hear the news

il regrette de ne pas avoir vu cette émission
he's sorry he didn't see this programme

tu as peur de ne pas avoir assez d'argent ?
are you worried you won't have enough money?

ii) **attendre** (to wait) and **douter** (to doubt):

j'attendrai d'avoir bu mon café
I'll wait until I've drunk my coffee

iii) most impersonal constructions:

il serait préférable de déclarer ces objets
it would be better to declare these things

il est important de garder votre billet
it's important that you should keep your ticket

iv) most conjunctions:

il est resté dans la voiture afin de ne pas se mouiller
he stayed in the car so as not to get wet

j'ai lu avant de m'endormir
I read before falling asleep

tu peux sortir, à condition de rentrer avant minuit
you can go out, as long as you're back before midnight

b) *à* + *infinitive replaces the subjunctive after:*

i) **de façon/manière**

mets la liste sur la table de manière à ne pas l'oublier
put the list on the table so that you won't forget it

ii) **premier, seul, dernier**

il a été le seul à s'excuser
he was the only one who apologised

) the infinitive without any linking preposition replaces the subjunctive after:

i) verbs of wishing and willing:

je voudrais sortir avec toi
I'd like to go out with you

ii) **il faut, il vaut mieux:**

il vous faudra prendre des chèques de voyage
you'll have to take some traveller's cheques

il lui a fallu recommencer à zéro
he had to start all over again

il vaudrait mieux lui apporter des fleurs que des bonbons
it would be better to take her flowers than sweets

Note: an indirect object pronoun is often used with **il faut** to indicate the subject (who has to do something).

iii) verbs of thinking:

je ne crois pas le connaître
I don't think I know him

tu penses être chez toi à cinq heures ?
do you think you'll be home at five?

iv) **pour** and **sans**:

le car est reparti sans nous attendre
the coach left without waiting for us

j'économise pour pouvoir acheter une moto
I'm saving up to buy a motorbike

8. THE CONDITIONAL

a) *The conditional present*

i) The conditional present is used to describe what someone would do or would be doing or what would happen (if something else were to happen):

si j'étais riche, j'*achèterais*** un château**
if I were rich, I *would buy* a castle

Note: when the main verb is in the conditional present, the verb after **si** is in the imperfect.

ii) It is also used in indirect questions or reported speech instead of the future:

il ne m'a pas dit s'il *viendrait*
he didn't tell me whether he *would come*

b) *The conditional perfect (or past conditional)*

The conditional perfect or past conditional is used to express what someone would have done or would have been doing or what would have happened:

si j'avais su, je n'aurais rien dit
if I had known, I wouldn't have said anything

qu'aurais-je fait sans toi ?
what would I have done without you?

Note: if the main verb is in the conditional perfect, the verb introduced by **si** is in the pluperfect.

c) *Tenses after si:*

The tense of the verb introduced by **si** is determined by the tense of the verb in the main clause:

MAIN VERB	VERB FOLLOWING 'SI'
conditional present →	imperfect
conditional perfect →	pluperfect

je te le dirais si je le savais
I would tell you if I knew

je te l'aurais dit si je l'avais su
I would have told you if I had known

Note: never use the conditional (or the future) with **si** unless **si** means whether (ie when it introduces an indirect question):

je me demande si j'y serais arrivé sans toi
I wonder if (= *whether*) I would have managed without you

4. THE IMPERATIVE

a) *Definition*

The imperative is used to give commands, or polite
instructions, or to make requests or suggestions; these can
be positive (affirmative imperative: 'do!') or negative ('don't!'):

mange ta soupe !	**n'aie pas peur !**
eat your soup	don't be afraid!
partons !	**entrez !**
let's go!	come in!
faites attention !	**n'hésitez pas !**
be careful!	don't hesitate!
tournez à droite à la poste	
turn right at the post office	

b) *Forms*

The imperative has only three forms, which are the same as the **tu**,
nous and **vous** forms of the present tense, but without the subject
pronoun:

	-ER VERBS	-IR VERBS	-RE VERBS
TU' FORM:	**regarde**	**choisis**	**attends**
	watch	choose	wait
NOUS' FORM:	**regardons**	**choisissons**	**attendons**
	let's watch	let's choose	let's wait
VOUS' FORM:	**regardez**	**choisissez**	**attendez**
	watch	choose	wait

Note:

i) the **-s** of the **tu** form of **-er** verbs is dropped, except when **y** or **en**
follow the verb:

parle-lui !	*But*	**parles-en avec lui**
speak to him!		speak to him about it
achète du sucre !	*But*	**achètes-en un kilo**
buy some sugar!		buy a kilo (of it)

ii) the distinction between the subject pronouns **tu** and **vous** (see p 70) applies to the **tu** and **vous** forms of the imperative:

> **prends ta sœur avec toi, Alain**
> take your sister with you, Alain

> **prenez le plat du jour, Monsieur ; c'est du poulet rôti**
> have today's set menu, sir; it's roast chicken

> **les enfants, prenez vos imperméables ; il va pleuvoir**
> take your raincoats, children; it's going to rain

c) *Negative commands*

In negative commands, the verb is placed between **ne** and **pas** (or the second part of other negative expressions):

> **ne fais pas ça !**   **ne dites rien !**
> don't do that!   don't say anything!

d) *Imperative with object pronouns*

In positive commands, object pronouns come after the verb and are attached to it by a hyphen. In negative commands, they come before the verb (see p 72, 74, 76 and 78):

> **dites-moi ce qui s'est passé**   **attendons-les !**
> tell me what happened   let's wait for them

> **prends-en bien soin, ne l'abîme pas !**
> take good care of it, don't damage it!

> **ne le leur dis pas !**   **ne les écoutez pas**
> don't tell them (that)!   don't listen to them

e) *Imperative of reflexive verbs*

The position of the reflexive pronoun of reflexive verbs is the same as that of object pronouns:

> **tais-toi !**   **levez-vous !**
> be quiet!   get up!

> **méfiez-vous de lui**   **arrêtons-nous ici**
> don't trust him   let's stop here

> **ne nous plaignons pas**   **ne t'approche pas plus !**
> let's not complain   don't come any closer!

Alternatives to the imperative

i) infinitive

the infinitive is often used instead of the imperative in written instructions and in recipes:

s'adresser au concierge
see the caretaker

ne pas fumer
no smoking

verser le lait et bien mélanger
pour in the milk and stir well

ii) subjunctive

as the imperative has no third person (singular or plural), **que** + subjunctive is used for giving orders in the third person:

que personne ne me dérange !
don't let anyone disturb me!

qu'il entre !
let him (come) in!

qu'elle parte, je m'en fiche !
I don't care if she goes!

Idiomatic usage

The imperative is used in spoken French in many set phrases. Here are some of the most common ones:

allons donc !
you don't say!

dis/dites donc !
by the way!
hey! (*protest*)

tiens/tenez !
here you are!

tiens ! voilà le facteur
ah! here comes the postman

tiens (donc) !
(oh) really?

tiens ! tiens !
well, well! (fancy that!)

voyons !
come (on) now!

voyons donc !
let's see now

H. THE INFINITIVE

1. The infinitive is the basic form of the verb. It is recognized by its ending, which is found in three forms corresponding to the three conjugations: **-er, -ir, -re**.

These endings give the verb the meaning 'to ....':

acheter	**choisir**	**vendre**
to buy	to choose	to sell

Note: although this applies as a general rule, the French infinitive will often be translated by a verb form in *-ing* (see p 240-1).

2. Uses of the infinitive

The infinitive can follow a preposition, a verb, a noun, a pronoun, an adverb or an adjective.

a) *After a preposition*

The infinitive can be used after some prepositions (**pour**, **avant de**, **sans**, **au lieu de**, **afin de** etc):

sans attendre	**avant de partir**
without waiting	before leaving

b) *After a verb*

There are three main constructions when a verb is followed by an infinitive:

> i) with no linking preposition
> ii) with the linking preposition **à**
> iii) with the linking preposition **de**

i) Verbs followed by the infinitive with no linking preposition:

★ verbs of wishing and willing, eg:

vouloir	to want
souhaiter	to wish
désirer	to wish, to want
espérer	to hope

voulez-vous manger maintenant ou plus tard ?
do you want to eat now or later?

je souhaite parler au directeur
I wish to speak to the manager

★ verbs of seeing, hearing and feeling, eg:

voir	to see
écouter	to listen to
regarder	to watch
sentir	to feel, to smell
entendre	to hear

je l'ai vu jouer	**tu m'as regardé danser ?**
I've seen him play	did you watch me dance?

j'ai entendu quelqu'un crier
I heard someone shout

★ verbs of motion, eg:

aller	to go
monter	to go/come up
venir	to come
entrer	to go/come in
rentrer	to go/come home
sortir	to go/come out
descendre	to go/come down

je viendrai te voir demain
I'll come and see you tomorrow

il est descendu laver la voiture
he went down to wash the car

va acheter le journal
go and buy the paper

Note: in English, 'to come' and 'to go' may be linked to the verb that follows by 'and'; 'and' is not translated in French.

aller + infinitive can be used to express a future action, eg what someone is going to do:

qu'est-ce que tu vas faire demain ?
what are you going to do tomorrow?

★ modal auxiliary verbs (see p 152-5)

★ verbs of liking and disliking, eg:

aimer	to like
adorer	to love
aimer mieux	to prefer
détester	to hate
préférer	to prefer

tu aimes voyager ?
do you like travelling?

j'aime mieux attendre
I'd rather wait

je déteste aller à la campagne
I hate going to the country

j'adore faire la grasse matinée
I love having a long lie

★ some impersonal verbs (see p 114-5)

★ a few other verbs, eg:

compter	to intend to
sembler	to seem
laisser	to let, to allow
faillir	'to nearly' (do)
oser	to dare

ils l'ont laissé partir
they let him go

je n'ose pas le lui demander
I daren't ask him

tu sembles être malade
you seem to be ill

je compte partir demain
I intend to leave tomorrow

j'ai failli manquer l'avion
I nearly missed the plane

★ in the following set expressions:

aller chercher	to go and get, to fetch
envoyer chercher	to send for
entendre dire (que)	to hear (that)
entendre parler de	to hear about
laisser tomber	to drop
venir chercher	to come and get
vouloir dire	to mean

va chercher ton argent
go and get your money

j'ai entendu dire qu'il était journaliste
I've heard that he is a journalist

tu as entendu parler de ce film ?
have you heard about this film?

ne le laisse pas tomber !
don't drop it!

ça veut dire "demain"
it means 'tomorrow'

ii) Verbs followed by **à** + infinitive

A list of these is given on p 190:

je dois aider ma mère à préparer le déjeuner
I must help my mother prepare lunch

il commence à faire nuit
it's beginning to get dark

alors, tu t'es décidé à y aller ?
so you've made up your mind to go?

je t'invite à venir chez moi pour les vacances de Noël
I invite you to come to my house for the Christmas holidays

je passe mon temps à lire et à regarder la télé
I spend my time reading and watching TV

cela sert à nettoyer les disques
this is used for cleaning records

iii) Verbs followed by **de** + infinitive

A list of these is given on p 191-2:

je crois qu'il s'est arrêté de pleuvoir
I think it's stopped raining

tu as envie de sortir ?
do you feel like going out?

le médecin a conseillé à Serge de rester au lit
the doctor advised Serge to stay in bed

j'ai décidé de rester chez moi
I decided to stay at home

essayons de faire du stop
let's try and hitch-hike

tu as fini de m'ennuyer ?
will you stop annoying me?

demande à Papa de t'aider
ask your Dad to help you

je t'interdis d'y aller
I forbid you to go

n'oublie pas d'en acheter !	**j'ai refusé de le faire**
don't forget to buy some!	I refused to do it
je vous prie de m'excuser	**il vient de téléphoner**
please forgive me	he's just phoned

c) *After a noun, a pronoun, an adverb or an adjective*

There are two possible constructions: with **à** or with **de**.

i) with the linking preposition **à**:

il avait plusieurs clients à voir
he had several customers to see

c'est difficile à dire
it's difficult to say

ii) with the linking preposition **de**:

je suis content de te voir
I am pleased to see you

iii) **à** or **de** with pronouns, adverbs or nouns?

★ **à** conveys the idea of something to do or to be done after the following:

beaucoup	a lot
plus	more
tant	so much
trop	too much
assez	enough
moins	less
rien	nothing
tout	everything
quelque chose	something

une maison à vendre	**j'ai des examens à préparer**
a house for sale	I've got exams to prepare

il nous a indiqué la route à suivre
he showed us the road to follow

il y a trop de livres à lire
there are too many books to read

il n'y a pas de temps à perdre
there's no time to lose

c'était une occasion à ne pas manquer
it was an opportunity not to be missed

★ **de** is used after nouns of an abstract nature, usually with the definite article, eg:

l'habitude de	the habit of
l'occasion de	the opportunity to
le temps de	the time to
le courage de	the courage to
l'envie de	the desire to
le besoin de	the need to
le plaisir de	the pleasure of
le moment de	the time to

il n'avait pas l'habitude d'être seul
he wasn't used to being alone

je n'ai pas le temps de lui parler
I don't have time to talk to him

avez-vous eu l'occasion de la rencontrer ?
did you have the opportunity to meet her?

ce n'est pas le moment de le déranger
now is not the time to disturb him

je n'ai pas eu le courage de le lui dire
I didn't have the courage to tell him

iv) **à** or **de** with adjectives?

★ **à** is used in a passive sense (something to be done) and after **c'est**:

un livre agréable à lire
a pleasant book to read

il est facile à satisfaire
he is easily satisfied

c'est intéressant à savoir
that's interesting to know

c'était impossible à faire
it was impossible to do

★ **de** is used after **il est** in an impersonal sense (see p 114):

> **il est intéressant de savoir que ...**
> it is interesting to know that ...

Note: for the use of **c'est** and **il est**, see p 242-3.

★ **de** is used after many adjectives, in particular those where the idea of 'of' is present in English, eg:

certain/sûr de	certain of/to
capable de	capable of
incapable de	incapable of
coupable de	guilty of

> **j'étais sûr de réussir**
> I was sure of succeeding

> **il est incapable d'y arriver seul**
> he is incapable of managing on his own

de is also used with adjectives of emotion, feeling and generally with adjectives denoting a state of mind, eg:

content de	pleased/happy to
surpris/étonné de	surprised to
fier de	proud to
heureux de	happy to
fâché de	annoyed to/at
triste de	sad to
gêné de	embarrassed to
désolé de	sorry for/to

> **j'ai été très content de recevoir ta lettre**
> I was very pleased to get your letter

> **elle sera surprise de vous voir**
> she will be surprised to see you

> **nous avons été très tristes d'apprendre la nouvelle**
> we were very sad to hear the news

But: **à** is used with **prêt à** (ready to) and **disposé à** (willing to):

> **es-tu prête à partir ?**
> are you ready to go?

> **je suis tout disposé à vous aider**
> I'm very willing to help you

d) **faire** + *infinitive*

faire is followed by an infinitive without any linking preposition to express the sense of 'having someone do something' or 'having something done'; two constructions are possible:

i) with one object
ii) with two objects

i) when only one object is used, it is a direct object:

> **je dois le faire réparer**
> I must have it fixed

> **il veut faire repeindre sa voiture**
> he wants to have his car resprayed

> **je ferai nettoyer cette veste ; je la ferai nettoyer**
> I'll have this jacket cleaned; I'll have it cleaned

> **tu m'as fait attendre !**　　**je le ferai parler**
> you made me wait!　　I'll make him talk

Note the following set expressions:

> **faire entrer**　　　　　　to show in
> **faire venir**　　　　　　 to send for

> **faites entrer ce monsieur**　　**je vais faire venir le docteur**
> show this gentleman in　　　　I'll send for the doctor

ii) when both **faire** and the following infinitive have an object, the object of **faire** is indirect:

> **elle lui a fait prendre une douche**
> she made him take a shower

> **je leur ai fait ranger leur chambre**
> I made them tidy their room

e) *Infinitive used as subject of another verb:*

> **trouver un emploi n'est pas facile**
> finding a job isn't easy

3. The perfect infinitive

a) *Form*

The perfect or past infinitive is formed with the infinitive of the
auxiliary **avoir** or **être** as appropriate (see p 106-8), followed by the
past participle of the verb, eg:

avoir mangé	**être allé**	**s'être levé**
to have eaten	to have gone	to have got up

b) *Use*

i) after the preposition **après** (after):

après avoir attendu une heure, il est rentré chez lui
after waiting for an hour, he went back home

il s'en est souvenu après s'être couché
he remembered after going to bed

ii) after certain verbs:

se souvenir de	to remember
remercier de	to thank for
regretter de	to regret, to be sorry for
être désolé de	to be sorry for

je vous remercie de m'avoir invité
I thank you for inviting me

il regrettait de leur avoir menti
he was sorry for lying to them

tu te souviens d'avoir fait cela ?
do you remember doing this ?

I. PARTICIPLES

1. The present participle

a) *Formation*

Like the imperfect, the present participle is formed by using the stem of the first person plural of the present tense (the **nous** form less the **-ons** ending):

-ons is replaced by **-ant** (= English *-ing*)

Exceptions:

INFINITIVE	PRESENT PARTICIPLE
avoir to have	**ayant** having
être to be	**étant** being
savoir to know	**sachant** knowing

b) *Use as an adjective*

Used as an adjective, the present participle agrees in number and in gender with its noun or pronoun:

un travail fatigant	**la semaine suivante**
tiring work	the following week
ils sont très exigeants	**des nouvelles surprenantes**
they're very demanding	surprising news

c) *Use as a verb*

The present participle is used far less frequently in French than in English, and English present participles in *-ing* are often not translated by a participle in French (see p 240-1).

i) used on its own, the present participle corresponds to the English present participle:

ne voulant plus attendre, ils sont partis sans moi
not wanting to wait any longer, they left without me

pensant bien faire, j'ai insisté
thinking I was doing the right thing, I insisted

ii) **en** + present participle

When the subject of the present participle is the same as that of the main verb, this structure is often used to express simultaneity (ie 'while doing something'), manner (ie 'by doing something') or to translate English phrasal verbs.

★ simultaneous actions

In English this structure is translated by:

- while/when/on + present participle (eg 'on arriving')
- while/when/as + subject + verb (eg 'as arrived')

il est tombé en descendant l'escalier
he fell as he was going down the stairs

en le voyant, j'ai éclaté de rire
when I saw him, I burst out laughing

elle lisait le journal en attendant l'autobus
she was reading the paper while waiting for the bus

Note: the adverb **tout** is often used before **en** to emphasize the fact that both actions are simultaneous, especially when there is an element of contradiction:

elle écoutait la radio tout en faisant ses devoirs
she was listening to the radio while doing her homework

tout en protestant, je les ai suivis
under protest, I followed them

★ manner

when expressing how an action is done, **en** + participle is translated by: 'by' + participle, eg:

il gagne sa vie en vendant des voitures d'occasion
he earns his living (by) selling second-hand cars

j'ai trouvé du travail en lisant les petites annonces
I found a job by reading the classified ads

★ phrasal verbs of motion

en + present participle is often used to translate English phrasal verbs expressing motion, where the verb expresses the means of motion and a preposition expresses the direction of movement (eg 'to run out', 'to swim across').

In French, the English preposition is translated by a verb, while the English verb is translated by **en** + present participle:

il est sorti du magasin *en courant*
he *ran* out of the shop

elle a traversé la route *en titubant*
she *staggered* across the road

2. The past participle

a) *Forms*

For the formation of the past participle see p 103.

b) *Use*

The past participle is mostly used as a verb in compound tenses or in the passive, but it can also be used as an adjective. In either case, there are strict rules of agreement to be followed.

c) *Rules of agreement of the past participle*

i) When it is used as an adjective, the past participle always agrees with the noun or pronoun it refers to:

un pneu crevé	**une pomme pourrie**
a burst tyre	a rotten apple
ils étaient épuisés	**trois assiettes cassées !**
they were exhausted	three broken plates!

Note: in French, the past participle is used as an adjective to describe postures or attitudes of the body, where English uses the present participle. The most common of these are:

accoudé	leaning on one's elbows
accroupi	squatting
agenouillé	kneeling
allongé	lying (down)
appuyé (contre)	leaning (against)
couché	lying (down)
étendu	lying (down)
penché	leaning (over)
(sus)pendu	hanging

il est allongé sur le lit	**une femme assise devant moi**
he's lying on the bed	a woman sitting in front of me

ii) In compound tenses:

★ with the auxiliary **avoir**:

the past participle only agrees in number and gender with the direct object when the direct object comes before the participle, ie in the following cases:

— in a clause introduced by the relative pronoun **que**:

> **le jeu-vidéo que j'ai acheté**   **la valise qu'il a perdue**
> the video-game I bought   the suitcase he lost

— with a direct object pronoun:

> **ta carte ? je l'ai reçue hier**
> your card? I got it yesterday

> **zut, mes lunettes ! je les ai laissées chez moi**
> blast, my glasses! I've left them at home

— in a clause introduced by **combien de**, **quel (quelle, quels, quelles)** or **lequel (laquelle, lesquels, lesquelles)**:

> **combien de pays as-tu visités ?**
> how many countries have you visited?

> **laquelle avez-vous choisie ?**
> which one did you choose?

Note: if the direct object comes after the past participle, the participle remains in the masculine singular form:

> **on a rencontré des gens très sympathiques**
> we met some very nice people

★ with the auxiliary **être**

— the past participle agrees with the subject of the verb:

> **quand est-elle revenue ?**   **elle était déjà partie**
> when did she come back?   she'd already left

> **ils sont passés te voir ?**   **elles sont restées là**
> did they come to see you?   they stayed here

Note: this rule also applies when the verb is in the passive:

> **elle a été arrêtée**
> she's been arrested

— reflexive verbs

in most cases, the past participle of reflexive verbs agrees with the reflexive pronoun if the pronoun is a direct object; since the reflexive pronoun refers to the subject, the number and gender of the past participle are determined by the subject:

> **Jacques s'est trompé**   **Marie s'était levée tard**
> Jacques made a mistake   Marie had got up late

ils se sont disputés ? **elles se sont vues**
did they have an argument? they saw each other

Michèle et Marie, vous vous êtes habillées ?
Michèle and Marie, have you got dressed yet?

But: the past participle does not agree when the reflexive pronoun is an indirect object:

elles se sont écrit
they wrote *to* each other

This is the case in particular where parts of the body are mentioned:

elle s'est lavé les cheveux **ils se sont serré la main**
she washed her hair they shook hands

J. THE PASSIVE

1. Formation

The passive is used when the subject does not perform the action, but is subjected to it, eg:

the house has been sold   he was made redundant

Passive tenses are formed with the corresponding tense of the verb 'être' ('to be', as in English), followed by the past participle of the verb, eg:

j'ai été invité
I was invited

The past participle must agree with its subject, eg:

elle a été renvoyée
she has been dismissed

ils seront déçus   **elles ont été vues**
they will be disappointed   they were seen

2. Avoidance of the passive

The passive is far less common in French than in English. In particular, an indirect object cannot become the subject of a sentence in French, ie the following sentence where 'he' is an indirect object has no equivalent in French:

he was given a book (*ie a book was given to him*)

In general, French tries to avoid the passive wherever possible. This can be done in several ways:

a) *Use of the pronoun on:*

on m'a volé mon portefeuille
my wallet has been stolen

on construit une nouvelle piscine
a new swimming pool is being built

en France, on boit beaucoup de vin
a lot of wine is drunk in France

b) *Agent becomes subject of the verb*

If the agent, ie the real subject, is mentioned in English, it can become the subject of the French verb:

> **la nouvelle va les surprendre**
> they will be surprised by *the news*

> **mon correspondent m'a invité**
> I've been invited by *my penfriend*

> **mon cadeau te plaît ?**
> are you pleased with *my present?*

c) *Use of a reflexive verb*

Reflexive forms can be created for a large number of verbs, particularly in the third person:

> **elle s'appelle Anne**
> she is called Anne

> **ton absence va se remarquer**
> your absence will be noticed

> **ce plat se mange froid**
> this dish is eaten cold

> **cela ne se fait pas ici**
> that isn't done here

d) *Use of se faire + infinitive (when the subject is a person):*

> **il s'est fait renverser par une voiture**
> he was run over by a car

> **je me suis fait voler (tout mon argent)**
> I've been robbed (of all my money)

3. Conjugation

For a complete conjugation table of a verb in the passive, see **être aimé** (to be loved) p 159.

K. MODAL AUXILIARY VERBS

The modal auxiliary verbs are always followed by the infinitive. They express an obligation, a probability, an intention, a possibility or a wish rather than a fact.

The five modal auxiliary verbs are: **DEVOIR, POUVOIR, SAVOIR, VOULOIR** and **FALLOIR**.

1. Devoir (conjugation see p 167)

Expresses: a) obligation, necessity
b) probability
c) intention, expectation

a) *obligation*

nous devons arriver à temps	**demain tu devras prendre le bus**
we must arrive in time	tomorrow you'll have to take the bus
nous avions dû partir	**j'ai dû avouer que j'avais tort**
we had (had) to go	I had to admit that I was wrong

In the conditional, **devoir** may be used for advice, ie to express what should be done (conditional present) or should have been done (past conditional):

vous devriez travailler davantage
you ought to/should work harder

tu ne devrais pas marcher sur l'herbe
you shouldn't walk on the grass

tu aurais dû tout avouer
you should have admitted everything

tu n'aurais pas dû manger ces champignons
you shouldn't have eaten those mushrooms

Note: the French infinitive is translated by a past participle in English:
manger = eat*en*.

b) *probability*

il doit être en train de dormir
he must be sleeping (he's probably sleeping)

j'ai dû me tromper de chemin
I must have taken the wrong road

Note: in a past narrative sequence in the distant past, 'must have' is translated by a pluperfect in French:

il dit qu'il avait dû se tromper de chemin
he said he must have taken the wrong road

c) *intention, expectation*

je dois aller chez le dentiste
I am supposed to go to the dentist's

le train doit arriver à 19h30
the train is due to arrive at 7.30 p.m.

2. Pouvoir (conjugation see p 179)

Expresses: a) capacity, ability
b) permission
c) possibility

a) *capacity/ability*

Superman peut soulever une maison
Superman can lift a house

cette voiture peut faire du 150
this car can go up to 93 mph

il était si faible qu'il ne pouvait pas sortir de son lit
he was so weak that he couldn't get out of bed

b) *permission*

puis-je entrer ?   **puis-je vous offrir du thé ?**
may I come in?   may I offer you some tea?

c) *possibility*

cela peut arriver
it can happen

Note: **pouvoir** + the infinitive is usually replaced by **peut-être** and the finite tense: eg **il s'est peut-être trompé de livres** (he may have taken the wrong books).

In the conditional, **pouvoir** is used to express something that could or might be (conditional present) or that could or might have been (past conditional):

> **tu pourrais t'excuser**
> you might apologize

> **j'aurais pu vous prêter mon magnétophone**
> I could have lent you my tape-recorder

Note: with verbs of perception (eg **entendre** to hear, **sentir** to feel, to smell, **voir** to see), **pouvoir** is often omitted:

> **j'entendais le bruit des vagues**
> I could hear the sound of the waves

3. Savoir (conjugation see p 182)

Means: 'to know how to'

> **je sais/savais conduire une moto**
> I can/used to be able to ride a motorbike

4. Vouloir (conjugation see p 188)

Expresses: a) desire
            b) wish
            c) intention

a) *desire*

> **je veux partir**   **voulez-vous danser avec moi ?**
> I want to go   will you dance with me?

b) *wish*

> **je voudrais être un lapin**
> I wish I were a rabbit

> **je voudrais trouver un travail intéressant**
> I should like to find an interesting job

> **j'aurais voulu lui donner un coup de poing**
> I would have liked to punch him

c) *intention*

il a voulu sauter par la fenêtre
he tried to jump out of the window

Note: **veuillez**, the imperative of **vouloir**, is used as a polite form to express a request ('would you please'):

veuillez ne pas déranger
please do not disturb

5. Falloir (conjugation see p 174)

Expresses: necessity

il faut manger pour vivre
you must eat to live

il faudrait manger plus tôt ce soir
we should eat earlier tonight

il aurait fallu apporter des sandwichs
we should have brought sandwiches

Note: some of the above verbs can also be used without infinitive constructions. They then take on a different meaning (eg **devoir** = to owe, **savoir** = to know).

L. CONJUGATION TABLES

The following verbs provide the main patterns of conjugation including the conjugation of the most common irregular verbs. They are arranged in alphabetical order:

-er verb *(see p 91)*	AIMER
-ir verb *(see p 91)*	FINIR
-re verb *(see p 91)*	VENDRE
Reflexive verb *(see p 109-12)*	SE MEFIER
Verb with auxiliary **être** *(see p 105-8)*	ARRIVER
Verb in the passive *(see p 150-1)*	ETRE AIME
Auxiliaries *(see p 103-8)*	AVOIR ETRE
Verb in **-eler/-eter** *(see p 97-8)*	APPELER
Verb in **e** + consonant + **er** *(see p 100)*	ACHETER
Verb in **é** + consonant + **er** *(see p 101-2)*	ESPERER
Modal auxiliaries *(see p 152-5)*	DEVOIR POUVOIR SAVOIR VOULOIR FALLOIR

Irregular verbs		
	ALLER	METTRE
	CONDUIRE	OUVRIR
	CONNAITRE	PRENDRE
	CROIRE	RECEVOIR
	DIRE	TENIR
	DORMIR	VENIR
	ECRIRE	VIVRE
	FAIRE	VOIR

'Harrap's French Verbs', a fully comprehensive list of French verbs and their conjugations, is also available in this series.

ACHETER to buy

PRESENT	IMPERFECT	FUTURE
j'achète	j'achetais	j'achèterai
tu achètes	tu achetais	tu achèteras
il achète	il achetait	il achètera
nous achetons	nous achetions	nous achèterons
vous achetez	vous achetiez	vous achèterez
ils achètent	ils achetaient	ils achèteront

PAST HISTORIC	PERFECT	PLUPERFECT
j'achetai	j'ai acheté	j'avais acheté
tu achetas	tu as acheté	tu avais acheté
il acheta	il a acheté	il avait acheté
nous achetâmes	nous avons acheté	nous avions acheté
vous achetâtes	vous avez acheté	vous aviez acheté
ils achetèrent	ils ont acheté	ils avaient acheté

CONDITIONAL

PAST ANTERIOR	PRESENT	PAST
j'eus acheté etc	j'achèterais	j'aurais acheté
	tu achèterais	tu aurais acheté
	il achèterait	il aurait acheté
	nous achèterions	nous aurions acheté
FUTURE PERFECT	vous achèteriez	vous auriez acheté
j'aurai acheté etc	ils achèteraient	ils auraient acheté

SUBJUNCTIVE

PRESENT	IMPERFECT	PERFECT
j'achète	j'achetasse	j'aie acheté
tu achetes	tu achetasses	tu aies acheté
il achète	il achetât	il ait acheté
nous achetions	nous achetássions	nous ayons acheté
vous achetiez	vous achetassiez	vous ayez acheté
ils achètent	ils achetassent	ils aient acheté

IMPERATIVE	INFINITIVE	PARTICIPLE
achète	**PRESENT**	**PRESENT**
achetons	acheter	achetant
achetez	**PAST**	**PAST**
	avoir acheté	acheté

AIMER   to like, to love

PRESENT	IMPERFECT	FUTURE
j'aime	j'aimais	j'aimerai
tu aimes	tu aimais	tu aimeras
il aime	il aimait	il aimera
nous aimons	nous aimions	nous aimerons
vous aimez	vous aimiez	vous aimerez
ils aiment	ils aimaient	ils aimeront

PAST HISTORIC	PERFECT	PLUPERFECT
j'aimai	j'ai aimé	j'avais aimé
tu aimas	tu as aimé	tu avais aimé
il aima	il a aimé	il avait aimé
nous aimâmes	nous avons aimé	nous avions aimé
vous aimâtes	vous avez aimé	vous aviez aimé
ils aimèrent	ils ont aimé	ils avaient aimé

	CONDITIONAL	
PAST ANTERIOR	**PRESENT**	**PAST**
j'eus aimé etc	j'aimerais	j'aurais aimé
	tu aimerais	tu aurais aimé
	il aimerait	il aurait aimé
	nous aimerions	nous aurions aimé
FUTURE PERFECT	vous aimeriez	vous auriez aimé
j'aurai aimé etc	ils aimeraient	ils auraient aimé

SUBJUNCTIVE

PRESENT	IMPERFECT	PERFECT
j'aime	j'aimasse	j'aie aimé
tu aimes	tu aimasses	tu aies aimé
il aime	il aimât	il ait aimé
nous aimions	nous aimassions	nous ayons aimé
vous aimiez	vous aimassiez	vous ayez aimé
ils aiment	ils aimassent	ils aient aimé

IMPERATIVE	*INFINITIVE*	*PARTICIPLE*
aime	**PRESENT**	**PRESENT**
aimons	aimer	aimant
aimez	**PAST**	**PAST**
	avoir aimé	aimé

ETRE AIME   to be loved

PRESENT	IMPERFECT	FUTURE
je suis aimé(e)	j'étais aimé(e)	je serai aimé(e)
tu es aimé(e)	tu étais aimé(e)	tu seras aimé(e)
il (elle) est aimé(e)	il (elle) était aimé(e)	il (elle) sera aimé(e)
nous sommes aimé(e)s	nous étions aimé(e)s	nous serons aimé(e)s
vous êtes aimé(e)(s)	vous étiez aimé(e)(s)	vous serez aimé(e)(s)
ils (elles) sont aimé(e)s	ils (elles) étaient aimé(e)s	ils (elles) seront aimé(e)s

PAST HISTORIC	PERFECT	PLUPERFECT
je fus aimé(e)	j'ai été aimé(e)	j'avais été aimé(e)
tu fus aimé(e)	tu as été aimé(e)	tu avais été aimé(e)
il (elle) fut aimé(e)	il (elle) a été aimé(e)	il (elle) avait été aimé(e)
nous fûmes aimé(e)s	nous avons été aimé(e)s	nous avions été aimé(e)s
vous fûtes aimé(e)(s)	vous avez été aimé(e)(s)	vous aviez été aimé(e)(s)
ils (elles) furent aimé(e)s	ils (elles) ont été aimé(e)s	ils (elles) avaient été aimé(e)s

CONDITIONAL

PAST ANTERIOR	PRESENT	PAST
j'eus été aimé(e) etc	je serais aimé(e)	j'aurais été aimé(e)
	tu serais aimé(e)	tu aurais été aimé(e)
	il (elle) serait aimé(e)	il (elle) aurait été aimé(e)
	nous serions aimé(e)s	nous aurions été aimé(e)s
FUTURE PERFECT	vous seriez aimé(e)(s)	vous auriez été aimé(e)(s)
j'aurai été aimé(e) etc	ils (elles) seraient aimé(e)s	ils (elles) auraient été aimé(e)s

SUBJUNCTIVE

PRESENT	IMPERFECT	PERFECT
je sois aimé(e)	je fusse aimé(e)	j'aie été aimé(e)
tu sois aimé(e)	tu fusses aimé(e)	tu aies été aimé(e)
il (elle) soit aimé(e)	il (elle) fût aimé(e)	il (elle) ait été aimé(e)
nous soyons aimé(e)s	nous fussions aimé(e)s	nous ayons été aimé(e)s
vous soyez aimé(e)(s)	vous fussiez aimé(e)(s)	vous ayez été aimé(e)(s)
ils (elles) soient aimé(e)s	ils (elles) fussent aimé(e)s	ils (elles) aient été aimé(e)s

IMPERATIVE	INFINITIVE	PARTICIPLE
sois aimé(e)	PRESENT	PRESENT
soyons aimé(e)s	être aimé(e)(s)	étant aimé(e)(s)
soyez aimé(e)(s)	PAST	PAST
	avoir été aimé(e)(s)	été aimé(e)(s)

ALLER to go

PRESENT	IMPERFECT	FUTURE
je vais	j'allais	j'irai
tu vas	tu allais	tu iras
il va	il allait	il ira
nous allons	nous allions	nous irons
vous allez	vous alliez	vous irez
ils vont	ils allaient	ils iront

PAST HISTORIC	PERFECT	PLUPERFECT
j'allai	je suis allé(e)	j'étais allé(e)
tu allas	tu es allé(e)	tu étais allé(e)
il alla	il est allé(e)	il était allé(e)
nous allâmes	nous sommes allé(e)s	nous étions allé(e)s
vous allâtes	vous êtes allé(e)(s)	vous étiez allé(e)(s)
ils allèrent	ils sont allé(e)s	ils étaient allé(e)s

	CONDITIONAL	
PAST ANTERIOR	PRESENT	PAST
je fus allé(e) etc	j'irais	je serais allé(e)
	tu irais	tu serais allé(e)
	il irait	il serait allé(e)
	nous irions	nous serions allé(e)s
FUTURE PERFECT	vous iriez	vous seriez allé(e)(s)
je serai allé(e) etc	ils iraient	ils seraient allé(e)s

SUBJUNCTIVE

PRESENT	IMPERFECT	PERFECT
j'aille	j'allasse	je sois allé(e)
tu ailles	tu allasses	tu sois allé(e)
il aille	il allât	il soit allé(e)
nous allions	nous allassions	nous soyons allé(e)s
vous alliez	vous allassiez	vous soyez allé(e)(s)
ils aillent	ils allassent	ils soient allé(e)s

IMPERATIVE	*INFINITIVE*	*PARTICIPLE*
va	PRESENT	PRESENT
allons	aller	allant
allez		
	PAST	PAST
	être allé(e)(s)	allé

APPELER to call

PRESENT	IMPERFECT	FUTURE
j'appelle	j'appelais	j'appellerai
tu appelles	tu appelais	tu appelleras
il appelle	il appelait	il appellera
nous appelons	nous appelions	nous appellerons
vous appelez	vous appeliez	vous appellerez
ils appellent	ils appelaient	ils appelleront

PAST HISTORIC	PERFECT	PLUPERFECT
j'appelai	j'ai appelé	j'avais appelé
tu appelas	tu as appelé	tu avais appelé
il appela	il a appelé	il avait appelé
nous appelâmes	nous avons appelé	nous avions appelé
vous appelâtes	vous avez appelé	vous aviez appelé
ils appelèrent	ils ont appelé	ils avaient appelé

CONDITIONAL

PAST ANTERIOR	PRESENT	PAST
j'eus appelé etc	j'appellerais	j'aurais appelé
	tu appellerais	tu aurais appelé
	il appellerait	il aurait appelé
	nous appellerions	nous aurions appelé
FUTURE PERFECT	vous appelleriez	vous auriez appelé
j'aurai appelé etc	ils appelleraient	ils auraient appelé

SUBJUNCTIVE

PRESENT	IMPERFECT	PERFECT
j'appelle	j'appelasse	j'aie appelé
tu appelles	tu appelasses	tu aies appelé
il appelle	il appelât	il ait appelé
nous appelions	nous appelassions	nous ayons appelé
vous appeliez	vous appelassiez	vous ayez appelé
ils appellent	ils appelassent	ils aient appelé

IMPERATIVE	INFINITIVE	PARTICIPLE
appelle	PRESENT	PRESENT
appelons	appeler	appelant
appelez	PAST	PAST
	avoir appelé	appelé

ARRIVER   to arrive, to happen

PRESENT	IMPERFECT	FUTURE
j'arrive	j'arrivais	j'arriverai
tu arrives	tu arrivais	tu arriveras
il arrive	il arrivait	il arrivera
nous arrivons	nous arrivions	nous arriverons
vous arrivez	vous arriviez	vous arriverez
ils arrivent	ils arriviaient	ils arriveront

PAST HISTORIC	PERFECT	PLUPERFECT
j'arrivai	je suis arrivé(e)	j'étais arrivé(e)
tu arrivas	tu es arrivé(e)	tu étais arrivé(e)
il arriva	il est arrivé(e)	il était arrivé(e)
nous arrivâmes	nous sommes arrivé(e)s	nous étions arrivé(e)s
vous arrivâtes	vous êtes arrivé(e)(s)	vous étiez arrivé(e)(s)
ils arrivèrent	ils sont arrivé(e)s	ils étaient arrivé(e)s

	CONDITIONAL	
PAST ANTERIOR	**PRESENT**	**PAST**
je fus arrivé(e) etc	j'arriverais	je serais arrivé(e)
	tu arriverais	tu serais arrivé(e)
	il arriverait	il serait arrivé(e)
FUTURE PERFECT	nous arriverions	nous serions arrivé(e)s
	vous arriveriez	vous seriez arrivé(e)(s)
je serai arrivé(e) etc	ils arriveraient	ils seraient arrivé(e)s

SUBJUNCTIVE

PRESENT	IMPERFECT	PERFECT
j'arrive	j'arrivasse	je sois arrivé(e)
tu arrives	tu arrivasses	tu sois arrivé(e)
il arrive	il arrivât	il soit arrivé(e)
nous arrivions	nous arrivassions	nous soyons arrivé(e)s
vous arriviez	vous arrivassiez	vous soyez arrivé(e)(s)
ils arrivent	ils arrivassent	ils soient arrivé(e)s

IMPERATIVE	*INFINITIVE*	*PARTICIPLE*
arrive	**PRESENT**	**PRESENT**
arrivons	arriver	arrivant
arrivez	**PAST**	**PAST**
	être arrivé(e)(s)	arrivé

AVOIR to have

PRESENT	IMPERFECT	FUTURE
j'ai	j'avais	j'aurai
tu as	tu avais	tu auras
il a	il avait	il aura
nous avons	nous avions	nous aurons
vous avez	vous aviez	vous aurez
ils ont	ils avaient	ils auront

PAST HISTORIC	PERFECT	PLUPERFECT
j'eus	j'ai eu	j'avais eu
tu eus	tu as eu	tu avais eu
il eut	il a eu	il avait eu
nous eûmes	nous avons eu	nous avions eu
vous eûtes	vous avez eu	vous aviez eu
ils eurent	ils ont eu	ils avaient eu

CONDITIONAL

PAST ANTERIOR	PRESENT	PAST
j'eus eu etc	j'aurais	j'aurais eu
	tu aurais	tu aurais eu
	il aurait	il aurait eu
	nous aurions	nous aurions eu
FUTURE PERFECT	vous auriez	vous auriez eu
j'aurai eu etc	ils auraient	ils auraient eu

SUBJUNCTIVE

PRESENT	IMPERFECT	PERFECT
j'aie	j'eusse	j'aie eu
tu aies	tu eusses	tu aies eu
il ait	il eût	il ait eu
nous ayons	nous eussions	nous ayons eu
vous ayez	vous eussiez	vous ayez eu
ils aient	ils eussent	ils aient eu

IMPERATIVE	INFINITIVE	PARTICIPLE
aie	PRESENT	PRESENT
ayons	avoir	ayant
ayez	PAST	PAST
	avoir eu	eu

CONDUIRE   to lead, to drive

PRESENT	IMPERFECT	FUTURE
je conduis	je conduisais	je conduirai
tu conduis	tu conduisais	tu conduiras
il conduit	il conduisait	il conduira
nous conduisons	nous conduisions	nous conduirons
vous conduisez	vous conduisiez	vous conduirez
ils conduisent	ils conduisaient	ils conduiront

PAST HISTORIC	PERFECT	PLUPERFECT
je conduisis	j'ai conduit	j'avais conduit
tu conduisis	tu as conduit	tu avais conduit
il conduisit	il a conduit	il avait conduit
nous conduisîmes	nous avons conduit	nous avions conduit
vous conduisîtes	vous avez conduit	vous aviez conduit
ils conduisirent	ils ont conduit	ils avaient conduit

CONDITIONAL

PAST ANTERIOR	PRESENT	PAST
j'eus conduit etc	je conduirais	j'aurais conduit
	tu conduirais	tu aurais conduit
	il conduirait	il aurait conduit
	nous conduirions	nous aurions conduit
FUTURE PERFECT	vous conduiriez	vous auriez conduit
j'aurai conduit etc	ils conduiraient	ils auraient conduit

SUBJUNCTIVE

PRESENT	IMPERFECT	PERFECT
je conduise	je conduisisse	j'aie conduit
tu conduises	tu conduisisses	tu aies conduit
il conduise	il conduisît	il ait conduit
nous conduisions	nous conduisissions	nous ayons conduit
vous conduisiez	vous conduisissiez	vous ayez conduit
ils conduisent	ils conduisissent	ils aient conduit

IMPERATIVE	INFINITIVE	PARTICIPLE
conduis	PRESENT	PRESENT
conduisons	conduire	conduisant
conduisez	PAST	PAST
	avoir conduit	conduit

CONNAITRE to know

PRESENT	IMPERFECT	FUTURE
je connais	je connaissais	je connaîtrai
tu connais	tu connaissais	tu connaîtras
il connaît	il connaissait	il connaîtra
nous connaissons	nous connaissions	nous connaîtrons
vous connaissez	vous connaissiez	vous connaîtrez
ils connaissent	ils connaissaient	ils connaîtront

PAST HISTORIC	PERFECT	PLUPERFECT
je connus	j'ai connu	j'avais connu
tu connus	tu as connu	tu avais connu
il connut	il a connu	il avait connu
nous connûmes	nous avons connu	nous avions connu
vous connûtes	vous avez connu	vous aviez connu
ils connurent	ils ont connu	ils avaient connu

	CONDITIONAL	
PAST ANTERIOR	PRESENT	PAST
j'eus connu etc	je connaîtrais	j'aurais connu
	tu connaîtrais	tu aurais connu
	il connaîtrait	il aurait connu
	nous connaîtrions	nous aurions connu
FUTURE PERFECT	vous connaîtriez	vous auriez connu
j'aurai connu etc	ils connaîtraient	ils auraient connu

SUBJUNCTIVE

PRESENT	IMPERFECT	PERFECT
je connaisse	je connusse	j'aie connu
tu connaisses	tu connusses	tu aies connu
il connaisse	il connût	il ait connu
nous connaissions	nous connussions	nous ayons connu
vous connaissiez	vous connussiez	vous ayez connu
ils connaissent	ils connussent	ils aient connu

IMPERATIVE	INFINITIVE	PARTICIPLE
connais	PRESENT	PRESENT
connaissons	connaître	connaissant
connaissez	PAST	PAST
	avoir connu	connu

CROIRE to believe

PRESENT	IMPERFECT	FUTURE
je crois	je croyais	je croirai
tu crois	tu croyais	tu croiras
il croit	il croyait	il croira
nous croyons	nous croyions	nous croirons
vous croyez	vous croyiez	vous croirez
ils croient	ils croyaient	ils croiront

PAST HISTORIC	PERFECT	PLUPERFECT
je crus	j'ai cru	j'avais cru
tu crus	tu as cru	tu avais cru
il crut	il a cru	il avait cru
nous crûmes	nous avons cru	nous avions cru
vous crûtes	vous avez cru	vous aviez cru
ils crurent	ils ont cru	ils avaient cru

CONDITIONAL

PAST ANTERIOR	PRESENT	PAST
j'eus cru etc	je croirais	j'aurais cru
	tu croirais	tu aurais cru
	il croirait	il aurait cru
	nous croirions	nous aurions cru
FUTURE PERFECT	vous croiriez	vous auriez cru
j'aurai cru etc	ils croiraient	ils auraient cru

SUBJUNCTIVE

PRESENT	IMPERFECT	PERFECT
je croie	je crusse	j'aie cru
tu croies	tu crusses	tu aies cru
il croie	il crût	il ait cru
nous croyions	nous crussions	nous ayons cru
vous croyiez	vous crussiez	vous ayez cru
ils croient	ils crussent	ils aient cru

IMPERATIVE	INFINITIVE	PARTICIPLE
crois	PRESENT	PRESENT
croyons	croire	croyant
croyez	PAST	PAST
	avoir cru	cru

DEVOIR to have to

PRESENT	IMPERFECT	FUTURE
je dois	je devais	je devrai
tu dois	tu devais	tu devras
il doit	il devait	il devra
nous devons	nous devions	nous devrons
vous devez	vous deviez	vous devrez
ils doivent	ils devaient	ils devront

PAST HISTORIC	PERFECT	PLUPERFECT
je dus	j'ai dû	j'avais dû
tu dus	tu as dû	tu avais dû
il dut	il a dû	il avait dû
nous dûmes	nous avons dû	nous avions dû
vous dûtes	vous avez dû	vous aviez dû
ils durent	ils ont dû	ils avaient dû

	CONDITIONAL	
PAST ANTERIOR	PRESENT	PAST
j'eus dû etc	je devrais	j'aurais dû
	tu devrais	tu aurais dû
	il devrait	il aurait dû
	nous devrions	nous aurions dû
FUTURE PERFECT	vous devriez	vous auriez dû
j'aurai dû	ils devraient	ils auraient dû

SUBJUNCTIVE

PRESENT	IMPERFECT	PERFECT
je doive	je dusse	j'aie dû
tu doives	tu dusses	tu aies dû
il doive	il dût	il ait dû
nous devions	nous dussions	nous ayons dû
vous deviez	vous dussiez	vous ayez dû
ils doivent	ils dussent	ils aient dû

IMPERATIVE	INFINITIVE	PARTICIPLE
dois	PRESENT	PRESENT
devons	devoir	devant
devez	PAST	PAST
	avoir dû	dû (due, dus)

DIRE to say

PRESENT	IMPERFECT	FUTURE
je dis	je disais	je dirai
tu dis	tu disais	tu diras
il dit	il disait	il dira
nous disons	nous disions	nous dirons
vous dites	vous disiez	vous direz
ils disent	ils disaient	ils diront

PAST HISTORIC	PERFECT	PLUPERFECT
je dis	j'ai dit	j'avais dit
tu dis	tu as dit	tu avais dit
il dit	il a dit	il avait dit
nous dîmes	nous avons dit	nous avions dit
vous dîtes	vous avez dit	vous aviez dit
ils dirent	ils ont dit	ils avaient dit

	CONDITIONAL	
PAST ANTERIOR	PRESENT	PAST
j'eus dit etc	je dirais	j'aurais dit
	tu dirais	tu aurais dit
	il dirait	il aurait dit
	nous dirions	nous aurions dit
FUTURE PERFECT	vous diriez	vous auriez dit
j'aurai dit etc	ils diraient	ils auraient dit

SUBJUNCTIVE

PRESENT	IMPERFECT	PERFECT
je dise	je disse	j'aie dit
tu dises	tu disses	tu aies dit
il dise	il dît	il ait dit
nous disions	nous dissions	nous ayons dit
vous disiez	vous dissiez	vous ayez dit
ils disent	ils dissent	ils aient dit

IMPERATIVE	*INFINITIVE*	*PARTICIPLE*
dis	PRESENT	PRESENT
disons	dire	disant
dites	PAST	PAST
	avoir dit	dit

DORMIR to sleep

PRESENT	IMPERFECT	FUTURE
je dors	je dormais	je dormirai
tu dors	tu dormais	tu dormiras
il dort	il dormait	il dormira
nous dormons	nous dormions	nous dormirons
vous dormez	vous dormiez	vous dormirez
ils dorment	ils dormaient	ils dormiront

PAST HISTORIC	PERFECT	PLUPERFECT
je dormis	j'ai dormi	j'avais dormi
tu dormis	tu as dormi	tu avais dormi
il dormit	il a dormi	il avait dormi
nous dormîmes	nous avons dormi	nous avions dormi
vous dormîtes	vous avez dormi	vous aviez dormi
ils dormirent	ils ont dormi	ils avaient dormi

CONDITIONAL

PAST ANTERIOR	PRESENT	PAST
j'eus dormi etc	je dormirais	j'aurais dormi
	tu dormirais	tu aurais dormi
	il dormirait	il aurait dormi
	nous dormirions	nous aurions dormi
FUTURE PERFECT	vous dormiriez	vous auriez dormi
j'aurai dormi etc	ils dormiraient	ils auraient dormi

SUBJUNCTIVE

PRESENT	IMPERFECT	PERFECT
je dorme	je dormisse	j'aie dormi
tu dormes	tu dormisses	tu aies dormi
il dorme	il dormît	il ait dormi
nous dormions	nous dormissions	nous ayons dormi
vous dormiez	vous dormissiez	vous ayez dormi
ils dorment	ils dormissent	ils aient dormi

IMPERATIVE	*INFINITIVE*	*PARTICIPLE*
dors	PRESENT	PRESENT
dormons	dormir	dormant
dormez	PAST	PAST
	avoir dormi	dormi

ECRIRE to write

PRESENT	IMPERFECT	FUTURE
j'écris	j'écrivais	j'écrirai
tu écris	tu écrivais	tu écriras
il écrit	il écrivait	il écrira
nous écrivons	nous écrivions	nous écrirons
vous écrivez	vous écriviez	vous écrirez
ils écrivent	ils écrivaient	ils écriront

PAST HISTORIC	PERFECT	PLUPERFECT
j'écrivis	j'ai écrit	j'avais écrit
tu écrivis	tu as écrit	tu avais écrit
il écrivit	il a écrit	il avait écrit
nous écrivîmes	nous avons écrit	nous avions écrit
vous écrivîtes	vous avez écrit	vous aviez écrit
ils écrivirent	ils ont écrit	ils avaient écrit

	CONDITIONAL	
PAST ANTERIOR	PRESENT	PAST
j'eus écrit etc	j'écrirais	j'aurais écrit
	tu écrirais	tu aurais écrit
	il écrirait	il aurait écrit
	nous écririons	nous aurions écrit
FUTURE PERFECT	vous écririez	vous auriez écrit
j'aurai écrit etc	ils écriraient	ils auraient écrit

SUBJUNCTIVE

PRESENT	IMPERFECT	PERFECT
j'écrive	j'écrivisse	j'aie écrit
tu écrives	tu écrivisses	tu aies écrit
il écrive	il écrivît	il ait écrit
nous écrivions	nous écrivissions	nous ayons écrit
vous écriviez	vous écrivissiez	vous ayez écrit
ils écrivent	ils écrivissent	ils aient écrit

IMPERATIVE	INFINITIVE	PARTICIPLE
écris	PRESENT	PRESENT
écrivons	écrire	écrivant
écrivez	PAST	PAST
	avoir écrit	écrit

ESPÉRER   to hope

PRESENT	IMPERFECT	FUTURE
j'espère	j'espérais	j'espérerai
tu espères	tu espérais	tu espéreras
il espère	il espérait	il espérera
nous espérons	nous espérions	nous espérerons
vous espérez	vous espériez	vous espérerez
ils espèrent	ils espéraient	ils espéreront

PAST HISTORIC	PERFECT	PLUPERFECT
j'espérai	j'ai espéré	j'avais espéré
tu espéras	tu as espéré	tu avais espéré
il espéra	il a espéré	il avait espéré
nous espérâmes	nous avons espéré	nous avions espéré
vous espérâtes	vous avez espéré	vous aviez espéré
ils espérèrent	ils ont espéré	ils avaient espéré

CONDITIONAL

PAST ANTERIOR	PRESENT	PAST
j'eus espéré etc	j'espérerais	j'aurais espéré
	tu espérerais	tu aurais espéré
	il espérerait	il aurait espéré
	nous espérerions	nous aurions espéré
FUTURE PERFECT	vous espéreriez	vous auriez espéré
j'aurai espéré etc	ils espéreraient	ils auraient espéré

SUBJUNCTIVE

PRESENT	IMPERFECT	PERFECT
j'espère	j'espérasse	j'aie espéré
tu espères	tu espérasses	tu aies espéré
il espère	il espérât	il ait espéré
nous espérions	nous espérassions	nous ayons espéré
vous espériez	vous espérassiez	vous ayez espéré
ils espèrent	ils espérassent	ils aient espéré

IMPERATIVE	INFINITIVE	PARTICIPLE
espère	**PRESENT**	**PRESENT**
espérons	espérer	espérant
espérez	**PAST**	**PAST**
	avoir espéré	espéré

ETRE to be

PRESENT	IMPERFECT	FUTURE
je suis	j'étais	je serai
tu es	tu étais	tu seras
il est	il était	il sera
nous sommes	nous étions	nous serons
vous êtes	vous étiez	vous serez
ils sont	ils étaient	ils seront

PAST HISTORIC	PERFECT	PLUPERFECT
je fus	j'ai été	j'avais été
tu fus	tu as été	tu avais été
il fut	il a été	il avait été
nous fûmes	nous avons été	nous avions été
vous fûtes	vous avez été	vous aviez été
ils furent	ils ont été	ils avaient été

CONDITIONAL

PAST ANTERIOR	PRESENT	PAST
j'eus été etc	je serais	j'aurais été
	tu serais	tu aurais été
	il serait	il aurait été
	nous serions	nous aurions été
FUTURE PERFECT	vous seriez	vous auriez été
j'aurai été etc	ils seraient	ils auraient été

SUBJUNCTIVE

PRESENT	IMPERFECT	PERFECT
je sois	je fusse	j'aie été
tu sois	tu fusses	tu aies été
il soit	il fût	il ait été
nous soyons	nous fussions	nous ayons été
vous soyez	vous fussiez	vous ayez été
ils soient	ils fussent	ils aient été

IMPERATIVE	INFINITIVE	PARTICIPLE
sois	**PRESENT**	**PRESENT**
soyons	être	étant
soyez	**PAST**	**PAST**
	avoir été	été

FAIRE to do, to make

PRESENT	IMPERFECT	FUTURE
je fais	je faisais	je ferai
tu fais	tu faisais	tu feras
il fait	il faisait	il fera
nous faisons	nous faisions	nous ferons
vous faites	vous faisiez	vous ferez
ils font	ils faisaient	ils feront

PAST HISTORIC	PERFECT	PLUPERFECT
je fis	j'ai fait	j'avais fait
tu fis	tu as fait	tu avais fait
il fit	il a fait	il avait fait
nous fîmes	nous avons fait	nous avions fait
vous fîtes	vous avez fait	vous aviez fait
ils firent	ils ont fait	ils avaient fait

CONDITIONAL

PAST ANTERIOR	PRESENT	PAST
j'eus fait etc	je ferais	j'aurais fait
	tu ferais	tu aurais fait
	il ferait	il aurait fait
	nous ferions	nous aurions fait
FUTURE PERFECT	vous feriez	vous auriez fait
j'aurai fait etc	ils feraient	ils auraient fait

SUBJUNCTIVE

PRESENT	IMPERFECT	PERFECT
je fasse	je fisse	j'aie fait
tu fasses	tu fisses	tu aies fait
il fasse	il fît	il ait fait
nous fassions	nous fissions	nous ayons fait
vous fassiez	vous fissiez	vous ayez fait
ils fassent	ils fissent	ils aient fait

IMPERATIVE	INFINITIVE	PARTICIPLE
fais	PRESENT	PRESENT
faisons	faire	faisant
faites	PAST	
	avoir fait	fait

FALLOIR to be necessary

PRESENT	IMPERFECT	FUTURE
il faut	il fallait	il faudra

PAST HISTORIC	PERFECT	PLUPERFECT
il fallut	il a fallu	il avait fallu

	CONDITIONAL	
PAST ANTERIOR	**PRESENT**	**PAST**
il eut fallu		
	il faudrait	il aurait fallu
FUTURE PERFECT		
il aura fallu		

SUBJUNCTIVE		
PRESENT	**IMPERFECT**	**PERFECT**
il faille	il fallût	il ait fallu

IMPERATIVE	*INFINITIVE*	*PARTICIPLE*
	PRESENT	**PRESENT**
	falloir	
	PAST	**PAST**
	avoir fallu	fallu

FINIR to finish

PRESENT	IMPERFECT	FUTURE
je finis	je finissais	je finirai
tu finis	tu finissais	tu finiras
il finit	il finissait	il finira
nous finissons	nous finissions	nous finirons
vous finissez	vous finissiez	vous finirez
ils finissent	ils finissaient	ils finiront

PAST HISTORIC	PERFECT	PLUPERFECT
je finis	j'ai fini	j'avais fini
tu finis	tu as fini	tu avais fini
il finit	il a fini	il avait fini
nous finîmes	nous avons fini	nous avions fini
vous finîtes	vous avez fini	vous aviez fini
ils finirent	ils ont fini	ils avaient fini

	CONDITIONAL	
PAST ANTERIOR	**PRESENT**	**PAST**
j'eus fini etc	je finirais	j'aurais fini
	tu finirais	tu aurais fini
	il finirait	il aurait fini
	nous finirions	nous aurions fini
FUTURE PERFECT	vous finiriez	vous auriez fini
j'aurai fini etc	ils finiraient	ils auraient fini

SUBJUNCTIVE

PRESENT	IMPERFECT	PERFECT
je finisse	je finisse	j'aie fini
tu finisses	tu finisses	tu aies fini
il finisse	il finît	il ait fini
nous finissions	nous finissions	nous ayons fini
vous finissiez	vous finissiez	vous ayez fini
ils finissent	ils finissent	ils aient fini

IMPERATIVE	INFINITIVE	PARTICIPLE
finis	**PRESENT**	**PRESENT**
finissons	finir	finissant
finissez	**PAST**	**PAST**
	avoir fini	fini

SE MEFIER to be suspicious

PRESENT	IMPERFECT	FUTURE
je me méfie	je me méfiais	je me méfierai
tu te méfies	tu te méfiais	tu te méfieras
il se méfie	il se méfiait	il se méfiera
nous nous méfions	nous nous méfiions	nous nous méfierons
vous vous méfiez	vous vous méfiiez	vous vous méfierez
ils se méfient	ils se méfiaient	ils se méfieront

PAST HISTORIC	PERFECT	PLUPERFECT
je me méfiai	je me suis méfié(e)	je m'étais méfié(e)
tu te méfias	tu t'es méfié(e)	tu t'étais méfié(e)
il se méfia	il s'est méfié(e)	il s'était méfié(e)
nous nous méfiâmes	nous ns. sommes méfié(e)s	nous ns. étions méfié(e)s
vous vous méfiâtes	vous vs. êtes méfié(e)(s)	vous vs. étiez méfié(e)(s)
ils se méfièrent	ils se sont méfié(e)s	ils s'étaient méfié(e)s

CONDITIONAL

PAST ANTERIOR	PRESENT	PAST
je me fus méfié(e) etc	je me méfierais	je me serais méfié(e)
	tu te méfierais	tu te serais méfié(e)
	il se méfierait	il se serait méfié(e)
	nous nous méfierions	nous ns. serions méfié(e)s
FUTURE PERFECT	vous vous méfieriez	vous vs. seriez méfié(e)(s)
je me serai méfié(e) etc	ils se méfieraient	ils se seraient méfié(e)s

SUBJUNCTIVE

PRESENT	IMPERFECT	PERFECT
je me méfie	je me méfiasse	je me sois méfié(e)
tu te méfies	tu te méfiasses	tu te sois méfié(e)
il se méfie	il se méfiât	il se soit méfié(e)
nous nous méfiions	nous nous méfiassions	nous ns. soyons méfié(e)s
vous vous méfiiez	vous vous méfiassiez	vous vs. soyez méfié(e)(s)
ils se méfient	ils se méfiassent	ils se soient méfié(e)s

IMPERATIVE	INFINITIVE	PARTICIPLE
méfie-toi	PRESENT	PRESENT
méfions-nous	se méfier	se méfiant
méfiez-vous	PAST	PAST
	s'être méfié(e)(s)	méfié

METTRE   to put

PRESENT	IMPERFECT	FUTURE
je mets	je mettais	je mettrai
tu mets	tu mettais	tu mettras
il met	il mettait	il mettra
nous mettons	nous mettions	nous mettrons
vous mettez	vous mettiez	vous mettrez
ils mettent	ils mettaient	ils mettront

PAST HISTORIC	PERFECT	PLUPERFECT
je mis	j'ai mis	j'avais mis
tu mis	tu as mis	tu avais mis
il mit	il a mis	il avait mis
nous mîmes	nous avons mis	nous avions mis
vous mîtes	vous avez mis	vous aviez mis
ils mirent	ils ont mis	ils avaient mis

CONDITIONAL

PAST ANTERIOR	PRESENT	PAST
j'eus mis etc	je mettrais	j'aurais mis
	tu mettrais	tu aurais mis
	il mettrait	il aurait mis
	nous mettrions	nous aurions mis
FUTURE PERFECT	vous mettriez	vous auriez mis
j'aurai mis etc	ils mettraient	ils auraient mis

SUBJUNCTIVE

PRESENT	IMPERFECT	PERFECT
je mette	je misse	j'aie mis
tu mettes	tu misses	tu aies mis
il mette	il mît	il ait mis
nous mettions	nous missions	nous ayons mis
vous mettiez	vous missiez	vous ayez mis
ils mettent	ils missent	ils aient mis

IMPERATIVE	INFINITIVE	PARTICIPLE
mets	PRESENT	PRESENT
mettons	mettre	mettant
mettez		
	PAST	PAST
	avoir mis	mis

OUVRIR to open

PRESENT	IMPERFECT	FUTURE
j'ouvre	j'ouvrais	j'ouvrirai
tu ouvres	tu ouvrais	tu ouvriras
il ouvre	il ouvrait	il ouvrira
nous ouvrons	nous ouvrions	nous ouvrirons
vous ouvrez	vous ouvriez	vous ouvrirez
ils ouvrent	ils ouvraient	ils ouvriront

PAST HISTORIC	PERFECT	PLUPERFECT
j'ouvris	j'ai ouvert	j'avais ouvert
tu ouvris	tu as ouvert	tu avais ouvert
il ouvrit	il a ouvert	il avait ouvert
nous ouvrîmes	nous avons ouvert	nous avions ouvert
vous ouvrîtes	vous avez ouvert	vous aviez ouvert
ils ouvrirent	ils ont ouvert	ils avaient ouvert

CONDITIONAL

PAST ANTERIOR	PRESENT	PAST
j'eus ouvert etc	j'ouvrirais	j'aurais ouvert
	tu ouvrirais	tu aurais ouvert
	il ouvrirait	il aurait ouvert
	nous ouvririons	nous aurions ouvert
FUTURE PERFECT	vous ouvririez	vous auriez ouvert
j'aurai ouvert etc	ils ouvriraient	ils auraient ouvert

SUBJUNCTIVE

PRESENT	IMPERFECT	PERFECT
j'ouvre	j'ouvrisse	j'aie ouvert
tu ouvres	tu ouvrisses	tu aies ouvert
il ouvre	il ouvrît	il ait ouvert
nous ouvrions	nous ouvrissions	nous ayons ouvert
vous ouvriez	vous ouvrissiez	vous ayez ouvert
ils ouvrent	ils ouvrissent	ils aient ouvert

IMPERATIVE	INFINITIVE	PARTICIPLE
	PRESENT	PRESENT
ouvre	ouvrir	ouvrant
ouvrons		
ouvrez	PAST	PAST
	avoir ouvert	ouvert

POUVOIR to be able to

PRESENT	IMPERFECT	FUTURE
je peux	je pouvais	je pourrai
tu peux	tu pouvais	tu pourras
il peut	il pouvait	il pourra
nous pouvons	nous pouvions	nous pourrons
vous pouvez	vous pouviez	vous pourrez
ils peuvent	ils pouvaient	ils pourront

PAST HISTORIC	PERFECT	PLUPERFECT
je pus	j'ai pu	j'avais pu
tu pus	tu as pu	tu avais pu
il put	il a pu	il avait pu
nous pûmes	nous avons pu	nous avions pu
vous pûtes	vous avez pu	vous aviez pu
ils purent	ils ont pu	ils avaient pu

CONDITIONAL

PAST ANTERIOR	PRESENT	PAST
j'eus pu etc	je pourrais	j'aurais pu
	tu pourrais	tu aurais pu
	il pourrait	il aurait pu
	nous pourrions	nous aurions pu
FUTURE PERFECT	vous pourriez	vous auriez pu
j'aurai pu etc	ils pourraient	ils auraient pu

SUBJUNCTIVE

PRESENT	IMPERFECT	PERFECT
je puisse	je pusse	j'aie pu
tu puisses	tu pusses	tu aies pu
il puisse	il pût	il ait pu
nous puissions	nous pussions	nous ayons pu
vous puissiez	vous pussiez	vous ayez pu
ils puissent	ils pussent	ils aient pu

IMPERATIVE	INFINITIVE	PARTICIPLE
	PRESENT	PRESENT
	pouvoir	pouvant
	PAST	PAST
	avoir pu	pu

PRENDRE to take

PRESENT	IMPERFECT	FUTURE
je prends	je prenais	je prendrai
tu prends	tu prenais	tu prendras
il prend	il prenait	il prendra
nous prenons	nous prenions	nous prendrons
vous prenez	vous preniez	vous prendrez
ils prennent	ils prenaient	ils prendront

PAST HISTORIC	PERFECT	PLUPERFECT
je pris	j'ai pris	j'avais pris
tu pris	tu as pris	tu avais pris
il prit	il a pris	il avait pris
nous prîmes	nous avons pris	nous avions pris
vous prîtes	vous avez pris	vous aviez pris
ils prirent	ils ont pris	ils avaient pris

CONDITIONAL

PAST ANTERIOR	PRESENT	PAST
j'eus pris etc	je prendrais	j'aurais pris
	tu prendrais	tu aurais pris
	il prendrait	il aurait pris
	nous prendrions	nous aurions pris
FUTURE PERFECT	vous prendriez	vous auriez pris
j'aurai pris etc	ils prendraient	ils auraient pris

SUBJUNCTIVE

PRESENT	IMPERFECT	PERFECT
je prenne	je prisse	j'aie pris
tu prennes	tu prisses	tu aies pris
il prenne	il prît	il ait pris
nous prenions	nous prissions	nous ayons pris
vous preniez	vous prissiez	vous ayez pris
ils prennent	ils prissent	ils aient pris

IMPERATIVE	INFINITIVE	PARTICIPLE
prends	PRESENT	PRESENT
prenons	prenant	
prenez		
	PAST	PAST
	avoir pris	pris

RECEVOIR to receive

PRESENT	IMPERFECT	FUTURE
je reçois	je recevais	je recevrai
tu reçois	tu recevais	tu recevras
il reçoit	il recevait	il recevra
nous recevons	nous recevions	nous recevrons
vous recevez	vous receviez	vous recevrez
ils reçoivent	ils recevaient	ils recevront

PAST HISTORIC	PERFECT	PLUPERFECT
je reçus	j'ai reçu	j'avais reçu
tu reçus	tu as reçu	tu avais reçu
il reçut	il a reçu	il avait reçu
nous reçûmes	nous avons reçu	nous avions reçu
vous reçûtes	vous avez reçu	vous aviez reçu
ils reçurent	ils ont reçu	ils avaient reçu

CONDITIONAL

	PRESENT	PAST
PAST ANTERIOR	je recevrais	j'aurais reçu
j'eus reçu etc	tu recevrais	tu aurais reçu
	il recevrait	il aurait reçu
	nous recevrions	nous aurions reçu
FUTURE PERFECT	vous recevriez	vous auriez reçu
j'aurai reçu etc	ils recevraient	ils auraient reçu

SUBJUNCTIVE

PRESENT	IMPERFECT	PERFECT
je reçoive	je reçusse	j'aie reçu
tu reçoives	tu reçusses	tu aies reçu
il reçoive	il reçût	il ait reçu
nous recevions	nous reçussions	nous ayons reçu
vous receviez	vous reçussiez	vous ayez reçu
ils reçoivent	ils reçussent	ils aient reçu

IMPERATIVE	INFINITIVE	PARTICIPLE
reçois	PRESENT	PRESENT
recevons	recevoir	recevant
recevez		
	PAST	PAST
	avoir reçu	reçu

SAVOIR to know

PRESENT	IMPERFECT	FUTURE
je sais	je savais	je saurai
tu sais	tu savais	tu sauras
il sait	il savait	il saura
nous savons	nous savions	nous saurons
vous savez	vous saviez	vous saurez
ils savent	ils savaient	ils sauront

PAST HISTORIC	PERFECT	PLUPERFECT
je sus	j'ai su	j'avais su
tu sus	tu as su	tu avais su
il sut	il a su	il avait su
nous sûmes	nous avons su	nous avions su
vous sûtes	vous avez su	vous aviez su
ils surent	ils ont su	ils avaient su

	CONDITIONAL	
PAST ANTERIOR	**PRESENT**	**PAST**
j'eus su etc	je saurais	j'aurais su
	tu saurais	tu aurais su
	il saurait	il aurait su
	nous saurions	nous aurions su
FUTURE PERFECT	vous sauriez	vous auriez su
j'aurai su etc	ils sauraient	ils auraient su

SUBJUNCTIVE

PRESENT	IMPERFECT	PERFECT
je sache	je susse	j'aie su
tu saches	tu susses	tu aies su
il sache	il sût	il ait su
nous sachions	nous sussions	nous ayons su
vous sachiez	vous sussiez	vous ayez su
ils sachent	ils sussent	ils aient su

IMPERATIVE	*INFINITIVE*	*PARTICIPLE*
sache	**PRESENT**	**PRESENT**
sachons	savoir	sachant
sachez	**PAST**	**PAST**
	avoir su	su

TENIR to hold

PRESENT	IMPERFECT	FUTURE
je tiens	je tenais	je tiendrai
tu tiens	tu tenais	tu tiendras
il tient	il tenait	il tiendra
nous tenons	nous tenions	nous tiendrons
vous tenez	vous teniez	vous tiendrez
ils tiennent	ils tenaient	ils tiendront

PAST HISTORIC	PERFECT	PLUPERFECT
je tins	j'ai tenu	j'avais tenu
tu tins	tu as tenu	tu avais tenu
il tint	il a tenu	il avait tenu
nous tînmes	nous avons tenu	nous avions tenu
vous tîntes	vous avez tenu	vous aviez tenu
ils tinrent	ils ont tenu	ils avaient tenu

CONDITIONAL

PAST ANTERIOR	PRESENT	PAST
j'eus tenu etc	je tiendrais	j'aurais tenu
	tu tiendrais	tu aurais tenu
	il tiendrait	il aurait tenu
	nous tiendrions	nous aurions tenu
FUTURE PERFECT	vous tiendriez	vous auriez tenu
j'aurai tenu etc	ils tiendraient	ils auraient tenu

SUBJUNCTIVE

PRESENT	IMPERFECT	PERFECT
je tienne	je tinsse	j'aie tenu
tu tiennes	tu tinsses	tu aies tenu
il tienne	il tînt	il ait tenu
nous tenions	nous tinssions	nous ayons tenu
vous teniez	vous tinssiez	vous ayez tenu
ils tiennent	ils tinssent	ils aient tenu

IMPERATIVE	INFINITIVE	PARTICIPLE
tiens	**PRESENT**	**PRESENT**
tenons	tenir	tenant
tenez	**PAST**	**PAST**
	avoir tenu	tenu

VENDRE to sell

PRESENT	IMPERFECT	FUTURE
je vends	je vendais	je vendrai
tu vends	tu vendais	tu vendras
il vend	il vendait	il vendra
nous vendons	nous vendions	nous vendrons
vous vendez	vous vendiez	vous vendrez
ils vendent	ils vendaient	ils vendront

PAST HISTORIC	PERFECT	PLUPERFECT
je vendis	j'ai vendu	j'avais vendu
tu vendis	tu as vendu	tu avais vendu
il vendit	il a vendu	il avait vendu
nous vendîmes	nous avons vendu	nous avions vendu
vous vendîtes	vous avez vendu	vous aviez vendu
ils vendirent	ils ont vendu	ils avaient vendu

CONDITIONAL

PAST ANTERIOR	PRESENT	PAST
j'eus vendu etc	je vendrais	j'aurais vendu
	tu vendrais	tu aurais vendu
	il vendrait	il aurait vendu
	nous vendrions	nous aurions vendu
FUTURE PERFECT	vous vendriez	vous auriez vendu
j'aurai vendu etc	ils vendraient	ils auraient vendu

SUBJUNCTIVE

PRESENT	IMPERFECT	PERFECT
je vende	je vendisse	j'aie vendu
tu vendes	tu vendisses	tu aies vendu
il vende	il vendît	il ait vendu
nous vendions	nous vendissions	nous ayons vendu
vous vendiez	vous vendissiez	vous ayez vendu
ils vendent	ils vendissent	ils aient vendu

IMPERATIVE	INFINITIVE	PARTICIPLE
vends	PRESENT	PRESENT
vendons	vendre	vendant
vendez	PAST	PAST
	avoir vendu	vendu

VENIR to come

PRESENT	IMPERFECT	FUTURE
je viens	je venais	je viendrai
tu viens	tu venais	tu viendras
il vient	il venait	il viendra
nous venons	nous venions	nous viendrons
vous venez	vous veniez	vous viendrez
ils viennent	ils venaient	ils viendront

PAST HISTORIC	PERFECT	PLUPERFECT
je vins	je suis venu(e)	j'étais venu(e)
tu vins	tu es venu(e)	tu étais venu(e)
il vint	il est venu(e)	il était venu(e)
nous vînmes	nous sommes venu(e)s	nous étions venu(e)s
vous vîntes	vous êtes venu(e)(s)	vous étiez venu(e)(s)
ils vinrent	ils sont venu(e)s	ils étaient venu(e)s

CONDITIONAL

PAST ANTERIOR	PRESENT	PAST
je fus venu(e) etc	je viendrais	je serais venu(e)
	tu viendrais	tu serais venu(e)
	il viendrait	il serait venu(e)
	nous viendrions	nous serions venu(e)s
FUTURE PERFECT	vous viendriez	vous seriez venu(e)(s)
je serai venu(e) etc	ils viendraient	ils seraient venu(e)s

SUBJUNCTIVE

PRESENT	IMPERFECT	PERFECT
je vienne	je vinsse	je sois venu(e)
tu viennes	tu vinsses	tu sois venu(e)
il vienne	il vînt	il soit venu(e)
nous venions	nous vinssions	nous soyons venu(e)s
vous veniez	vous vinssiez	vous soyez venu(e)(s)
ils viennent	ils vinssent	ils soient venu(e)s

IMPERATIVE	*INFINITIVE*	*PARTICIPLE*
viens	**PRESENT**	**PRESENT**
venons	venir	venant
venez	**PAST**	**PAST**
	être venu(e)(s)	venu

VIVRE to live

PRESENT	**IMPERFECT**	**FUTURE**
je vis	je vivais	je vivrai
tu vis	tu vivais	tu vivras
il vit	il vivait	il vivra
nous vivons	nous vivions	nous vivrons
vous vivez	vous viviez	vous vivrez
ils vivent	ils vivaient	ils vivront

PAST HISTORIC	**PERFECT**	**PLUPERFECT**
je vécus	j'ai vécu	j'avais vécu
tu vécus	tu as vécu	tu avais vécu
il vécut	il a vécu	il avait vécu
nous vécûmes	nous avons vécu	nous avions vécu
vous vécûtes	vous avez vécu	vous aviez vécu
ils vécurent	ils ont vécu	ils avaient vécu

	CONDITIONAL	
PAST ANTERIOR	**PRESENT**	**PAST**
j'eus vécu etc	je vivrais	j'aurais vécu
	tu vivrais	tu aurais vécu
	il vivrait	il aurait vécu
	nous vivrions	nous aurions vécu
FUTURE PERFECT	vous vivriez	vous auriez vécu
j'aurai vécu etc	ils vivraient	ils auraient vécu

SUBJUNCTIVE

PRESENT	**IMPERFECT**	**PERFECT**
je vive	je vécusse	j'aie vécu
tu vives	tu vécusses	tu aies vécu
il vive	il vécût	il ait vécu
nous vivions	nous vécussions	nous ayons vécu
vous viviez	vous vécussiez	vous ayez vécu
ils vivent	ils vécussent	ils aient vécu

IMPERATIVE	*INFINITIVE*	*PARTICIPLE*
vis	**PRESENT**	**PRESENT**
vivons	vivre	vivant
vivez	**PAST**	**PAST**
	avoir vécu	vécu

VOIR to see

PRESENT	IMPERFECT	FUTURE
je vois	je voyais	je verrai
tu vois	tu voyais	tu verras
il voit	il voyait	il verra
nous voyons	nous voyions	nous verrons
vous voyez	vous voyiez	vous verrez
ils voient	ils voyaient	ils verront

PAST HISTORIC	PERFECT	PLUPERFECT
je vis	j'ai vu	j'avais vu
tu vis	tu as vu	tu avais vu
il vit	il a vu	il avait vu
nous vîmes	nous avons vu	nous avions vu
vous vîtes	vous avez vu	vous aviez vu
ils virent	ils ont vu	ils avaient vu

CONDITIONAL

PAST ANTERIOR	PRESENT	PAST
j'eus vu etc	je verrais	j'aurais vu
	tu verrais	tu aurais vu
	il verrait	il aurait vu
	nous verrions	nous aurions vu
FUTURE PERFECT	vous verriez	vous auriez vu
j'aurai vu etc	ils verraient	ils auraient vu

SUBJUNCTIVE

PRESENT	IMPERFECT	PERFECT
je voie	je visse	j'aie vu
tu voies	tu visses	tu aies vu
il voie	il vît	il ait vu
nous voyions	nous vissions	nous ayons vu
vous voyiez	vous vissiez	vous ayez vu
ils voient	ils vissent	ils aient vu

IMPERATIVE	*INFINITIVE*	*PARTICIPLE*
vois	**PRESENT**	**PRESENT**
voyons	voir	voyant
voyez	**PAST**	**PAST**
	avoir vu	vu

VOULOIR to want

PRESENT	IMPERFECT	FUTURE
je veux	je voulais	je voudrai
tu veux	tu voulais	tu voudras
il veut	il voulait	il voudra
nous voulons	nous voulions	nous voudrons
vous voulez	vous vouliez	vous voudrez
ils veulent	ils voulaient	ils voudront

PAST HISTORIC	PERFECT	PLUPERFECT
je voulus	j'ai voulu	j'avais voulu
tu voulus	tu as voulu	tu avais voulu
il voulut	il a voulu	il avait voulu
nous voulûmes	nous avons voulu	nous avions voulu
vous voulûtes	vous avez voulu	vous aviez voulu
ils voulurent	ils ont voulu	ils avaient voulu

	CONDITIONAL	
PAST ANTERIOR	**PRESENT**	**PAST**
j'eus voulu etc	je voudrais	j'aurais voulu
	tu voudrais	tu aurais voulu
	il voudrait	il aurait voulu
	nous voudrions	nous aurions voulu
FUTURE PERFECT	vous voudriez	vous auriez voulu
j'aurai voulu etc	ils voudraient	ils auraient voulu

SUBJUNCTIVE

PRESENT	IMPERFECT	PERFECT
je veuille	je voulusse	j'aie voulu
tu veuilles	tu voulusses	tu aies voulu
il veuille	il voulût	il ait voulu
nous voulions	nous voulussions	nous ayons voulu
vous vouliez	vous voulussiez	vous ayez voulu
ils veuillent	ils voulussent	ils aient voulu

IMPERATIVE	*INFINITIVE*	*PARTICIPLE*
veuille	**PRESENT**	**PRESENT**
veuillons	vouloir	voulant
veuillez	**PAST**	**PAST**
	avoir voulu	voulu

M. VERB CONSTRUCTIONS

There are two main types of verb constructions: verbs can be followed:

1. by another verb in the infinitive
2. by an object (a noun or a pronoun)

1. Verbs followed by an infinitive

There are three main constructions when a verb is followed by an infinitive:

a) verb + infinitive (without any linking preposition)
b) verb + **à** + infinitive
c) verb + **de** + infinitive

For examples of these three types of constructions, see p 136-40 and 143-4.

a) *Verbs followed by an infinitive without preposition*

These include verbs of wishing and willing, of movement and of perception:

adorer	**aimer**	**aimer mieux**
to love	to like	to prefer
aller	**compter**	**descendre**
to go (and)	to intend to	to go down (and)
désirer	**détester**	**devoir**
to wish	to hate	to have to
écouter	**entendre**	**entrer**
to listen to	to hear	to go in (and)
envoyer	**espérer**	**faire**
to send	to hope to	to make
falloir	**laisser**	**monter**
to have to	to let	to go up (and)
oser	**pouvoir**	**préférer**
to dare	to be able to	to prefer to
regarder	**rentrer**	**savoir**
to watch	to go in/back (and)	to know how to
sembler	**sentir**	**sortir**
to seem to	to feel	to go out (and)

souhaiter	**valoir mieux**	**venir**
to wish to	to be better to	to come (and)
voir	**vouloir**	
to see	to want to	

b) *Verbs followed by* **à** + *infinitive*

aider à	to help (to do)
s'amuser à	to enjoy (doing)
apprendre à	to learn (to do)
s'apprêter à	to get ready (to do)
arriver à	to manage (to do)
s'attendre à	to expect (to do)
autoriser à	to allow (to do)
chercher à	to try (to do)
commencer à	to start (doing)
consentir à	to agree (to do)
consister à	to consist in (doing)
continuer à	to continue (to do)
se décider à	to make up one's mind (to do)
encourager à	to encourage (to do)
enseigner à	to teach how (to do)
forcer à	to force (to do)
s'habituer à	to get used (to doing)
hésiter à	to hesitate (to do)
inciter à	to prompt (to do)
s'intéresser à	to be interested in (doing)
inviter à	to invite (to do)
se mettre à	to start (doing)
obliger à	to force (to do)
parvenir à	to succeed (in doing)
passer son temps à	to spend one's time (doing)
perdre son temps à	to waste one's time (doing)
persister à	to persist in (doing)
pousser à	to urge (to do)
se préparer à	to get ready (to do)
renoncer à	to give up (doing)
rester à	to be left (to do)
réussir à	to manage (to do)
servir à	to be used for (doing)
songer à	to think of (doing)
tarder à	to delay/be late in (doing)
tenir à	to be keen (to do)

c) *Verbs followed by* **de** + *infinitive:*

accepter de	to agree (to do)
accuser de	to accuse of (doing)
achever de	to finish (doing)
s'arrêter de	to stop (doing)
avoir besoin de	to need (to do)
avoir envie de	to feel like (doing)
avoir peur de	to be afraid (to do)
cesser de	to stop (doing)
se charger de	to undertake (to do)
commander de	to order (to do)
conseiller de	to advise (to do)
se contenter de	to make do with (doing)
craindre de	to be afraid (to do)
décider de	to decide (to do)
déconseiller de	to advise against (doing)
défendre de	to forbid (to do)
demander de	to ask (to do)
se dépêcher de	to hasten (to do)
dire de	to tell (to do)
dissuader de	to dissuade from (doing)
s'efforcer de	to strive (to do)
empêcher de	to prevent (from doing)
s'empresser de	to hasten (to do)
entreprendre de	to undertake (to do)
essayer de	to try (to do)
s'étonner de	to be surprised (at doing)
éviter de	to avoid (doing)
s'excuser de	to apologize for (doing)
faire semblant de	to pretend (to do)
feindre de	to pretend (to do)
finir de	to finish (doing)
se garder de	to be careful not to (do)
se hâter de	to hasten (to do)
interdire de	to forbid (to do)
jurer de	to swear (to do)
manquer de	'to nearly' (do)
menacer de	to threaten (to do)
mériter de	to deserve (to do)
négliger de	to fail (to do)
s'occuper de	to undertake (to do)
offrir de	to offer (to do)

omettre de	to omit (to do)
ordonner de	to order (to do)
oublier de	to forget (to do)
permettre de	to allow (to do)
persuader de	to persuade (to do)
prier de	to ask (to do)
promettre de	to promise (to do)
proposer de	to offer (to do)
recommander de	to recommend (to do)
refuser de	to refuse (to do)
regretter de	to be sorry (to do)
remercier de	to thank for (doing)
résoudre de	to resolve (to do)
risquer de	to risk (doing)
se souvenir de	to remember (doing)
suggérer de	to suggest (doing)
supplier de	to implore (to do)
tâcher de	to try (to do)
tenter de	to try (to do)
venir de	to have just (done)

2. Verbs followed by an object

In general, verbs which take a direct object in French also take a direct object in English, and verbs which take an indirect object in French (ie verb + preposition + object) also take an indirect object in English.

There are however some exceptions:

a) *Verbs followed by an indirect object in English but not in French* (the English preposition is not translated):

attendre	to wait for
chercher	to look for
demander	to ask for
écouter	to listen to
espérer	to hope for
payer	to pay for
regarder	to look at
reprocher	to blame for

on a demandé l'addition	**j'attendais l'autobus**
we asked for the bill	I was waiting for the bus
je cherche mon frère	**tu écoutes la radio ?**
I'm looking for my brother	are you listening to the radio?

b) *Verbs which take a direct object in English, but an indirect object in French:*

convenir à	to suit
se fier à	to trust
jouer à	to play (*game, sport*)
jouer de	to play (*musical instrument*)
obéir à	to obey
désobéir à	to disobey
pardonner à	to forgive
renoncer à	to give up
répondre à	to answer
résister à	to resist
ressembler à	to resemble (to look like)
téléphoner à	to phone

tu peux te fier à moi
you can trust me

tu joues souvent au tennis ?
do you often play tennis?

il joue bien de la guitare
he plays the guitar well

tu as répondu à sa lettre ?
did you answer his letter?

téléphonons au médecin
let's phone the doctor

obéis à ton père !
obey your father!

c) *Verbs which take a direct object in English but de + indirect object in French:*

s'apercevoir de	to notice
s'approcher de	to come near
avoir besoin de	to need
changer de	to change
douter de	to doubt
se douter de	to suspect
s'emparer de	to seize, to grab
jouir de	to enjoy
manquer de	to lack, to miss
se méfier de	to mistrust
se servir de	to use
se souvenir de	to remember
se tromper de ...	to get the wrong ...

je dois changer de train ?
do I have to change trains?

il ne s'est aperçu de rien
he didn't notice anything

méfiez-vous de lui
don't trust him

je me servirai de ton vélo
I'll use your bike

tu te souviens de Jean ?
do you remember Jean?

il s'est trompé de numéro
he got the wrong number

d) *Some verbs take à or de before an object, whereas their English equivalent uses a different preposition:*

i) Verb + **à** + object:

croire à	to believe in
s'intéresser à	to be interested in
penser à	to think of/about
songer à	to think of
rêver à	to dream of/about
servir à	to be used for

je m'intéresse au football et à la course automobile
I'm interested in football and in motor-racing

à quoi penses-tu ?
what are you thinking about?

ça sert à quoi ?
what is this used for?

ii) Verb + **de** + object:

dépendre de	to depend on
être fâché de	to be annoyed at
féliciter de	to congratulate for
parler de	to speak of/about
remercier de	to thank for
rire de	to laugh at
traiter de	to deal with, to be about
vivre de	to live on

cela dépendra du temps
it'll depend on the weather

il m'a parlé de toi
he told me about you

tu l'as remercié du cadeau qu'il t'a fait ?
did you thank him for the present he gave you?

3. Verbs followed by one direct object and one indirect object

a) In general, these are verbs of giving or lending, and their English equivalents are constructed in the same way, eg:

donner quelque chose à quelqu'un
to give something to someone

il a vendu son ordinateur à son voisin
he sold his computer to his neighbour

Note: After such verbs, the preposition 'to' is often omitted in English but **à** cannot be omitted in French, and particular care must be taken when object pronouns are used with these verbs (see p 73).

) With verbs expressing 'taking away', **à** is translated by 'from' (**qn** stands for 'quelqu'un' and **sb** for 'somebody'):

acheter à qn	to buy from sb
cacher à qn	to hide from sb
demander à qn	to ask sb for
emprunter à qn	to borrow from sb
enlever à qn	to take away from sb
ôter à qn	to take away from sb
prendre à qn	to take from sb
voler à qn	to steal from sb

à qui as-tu emprunté cela ?
who did you borrow this from?

il l'a volé à son frère
he stole it from his brother

4. Verb + indirect object + de + infinitive

Some verbs which take a direct object in English are followed by **à** + object + **de** + infinitive in French (**qn** stands for 'quelqu'un' and **sb** for 'somebody'):

commander à qn de faire	to order sb to do
conseiller à qn de faire	to advise sb to do
défendre à qn de faire	to forbid sb to do
demander à qn de faire	to ask sb to do
dire à qn de faire	to tell sb to do
ordonner à qn de faire	to order sb to do
permettre à qn de faire	to allow sb to do
promettre à qn de faire	to promise sb to do
proposer à qn de faire	to offer to do for sb,
	to suggest to sb to do

je lui ai conseillé de ne pas essayer
I advised him not to try

demande à ton fils de t'aider
ask your son to help you

j'ai promis à mes parents de ne jamais recommencer
I promised my parents never to do this again

8. PREPOSITIONS

Prepositions in both French and English can have many different meanings, which presents considerable difficulties for the translator. The following guide to the most common prepositions sets out the generally accepted meanings on the left, with a description of their use in brackets, and an illustration. The main meanings are given first. Prepositions are listed in alphabetical order.

à

at	(place)	**au troisième arrêt** at the third stop
	(date)	**à Noël** at Christmas
	(time)	**à trois heures** at three o'clock
	(idiom)	**au hasard, au travail** at random, at work
in	(place)	**à Montmartre** in Montmartre **à Lyon** in Lyons **au supermarché** in the supermarket **à la campagne** in the country **au lit** in bed **au loin** in the distance
	(manner)	**à la française** in the French way **à ma façon** (in) my way

o	(place)	**aller au théâtre** to go to the theatre **aller à Londres** to go to London
	(+ infinitive)	**c'est facile à faire** it is easy to do (*see p 140*)
way from	(distance)	**à 3 km d'ici** three kms away
by	(means)	**aller à bicyclette/à vélo** to go by bike **je l'ai reconnu à ses habits** I recognized him by his clothing
	(manner)	**fait à la main** made by hand
	(rate)	**à la centaine** by the hundred **100 km à l'heure** 60 mph
for/up to	(+ pronoun)	**c'est à vous de jouer** it's your turn **c'est à nous de le lui dire** it's up to us to tell him
	(purpose)	**une tasse à café** a coffee cup
his/her/my etc	(possessive)	**son sac à elle** her bag
on	(means)	**aller à cheval/à pied** to go on horseback/on foot
	(place)	**à la page 12** on page 12 **à droite/à gauche** on/to the right/left
	(time)	**à cette occasion** on this occasion

with	(descriptive)	**une maison à cinq pièces**
		a house with five rooms
		un homme aux cheveux blonds
		a man with blond hair
		l'homme à la valise
		the man with the case
	(idiom)	**à bras ouverts**
		with open arms

For the use of the preposition à with the infinitive see verb constructions p 190.

après

after	(time)	**après votre arrivée**
		after your arrival
	(sequence)	**24 ans après la mort du président**
		24 years after the death of the President
		après avoir/être *(see p 144)*

auprès de

near		**assieds-toi auprès de moi**
		sit down near me
compared to		**ce n'est rien auprès de ce que tu as fait**
		it's nothing compared to what you've done

avant

before	(time)	**avant cet après-midi**
		before this afternoon
		avant ce soir
		before tonight
		avant de s'asseoir
		before sitting down
	(preference)	**la famille avant tout**
		the family first (before everything)

avec

with	(association)	**aller avec lui** to go with him
	(means)	**il a tondu le gazon avec une tondeuse** he cut the lawn with a lawnmower

chez

at	(place)	**chez moi/toi** at/to my/your house **chez mon oncle** at my uncle's **chez le pharmacien** at the chemist's
among		**chez les Ecossais** among the Scots
about		**ce qui m'énerve chez toi, c'est …** what annoys me about you is …
in		**chez Sartre** in Sartre's work

contre

against	(place)	**contre le mur** against the wall
with	(after verb)	**je suis fâché contre elle** I'm angry with her
for		**échanger des gants contre un foulard** to exchange gloves for a scarf

dans

in	(position)	**dans ma serviette** in my briefcase
	(time)	**je pars dans deux jours** I'm leaving in two days' time
	(idiom)	**dans l'attente de vous voir** looking forward to seeing you
from	(idiom)	**prendre quelque chose dans l'armoire** to take something from the cupboard
on	(idiom)	**dans le train** on the train
out of	(idiom)	**boire dans un verre** to drink out of a glass

de

from	(place)	**je suis venu de Glasgow** I have come from Glasgow
	(date)	**du 5 février au 10 mars** from February 5th to March 10th **d'un weekend à l'autre** from one weekend to another
of	(adjectival)	**un cri de triomphe** a shout of triumph
	(contents)	**une tasse de café** a cup of coffee
	(cause)	**mourir de faim** to die of hunger
	(measurement)	**long de 3 mètres** 3 metres long
	(time)	**ma montre retarde de 10 minutes** my watch is 10 minutes slow
	(price)	**le montant est de 200 francs** the total is 200 francs

	(possessive)	**la mini-jupe de ma sœur** my sister's miniskirt
	(adjectival)	**les vacances de Pâques** the Easter holidays
	(after 'quelque chose')	**quelque chose de bon** something good
	(after 'rien')	**rien de nouveau** nothing new
	(after 'personne')	**personne d'autre** nobody else
	(quantity)	**beaucoup de, peu de** many, few
by	(idiom)	**je le connais de vue** I know him by sight
in	(manner)	**de cette façon** in this way
	(after superlatives)	**la plus haute montagne d'Ecosse** the highest mountain in Scotland
on	(position)	**de ce côté** on this side
than	(comparative)	**moins de 5 francs** less than 5 francs **plus de trois litres** more than three litres
to	(after adjectives)	**ravi de vous voir** delighted to see you **il est facile de le faire** it is easy to do it
	(after verbs)	**s'efforcer de** to try to
with	(cause)	**tomber de fatigue** to drop with exhaustion

depuis

for	(time)	**j'étudie le français depuis 3 ans**
		I have been studying French for 3 years
		j'étudiais le français depuis 3 ans
		I had been studying French for 3 years
		je n'ai pas vu de lapins depuis des années
		I haven't seen a rabbit for years
from	(place)	**depuis ma fenêtre, je vois la mer**
		from my window I can see the sea
	(time)	**depuis le matin jusqu'au soir**
		from morning till evening
since		**depuis dimanche**
		since Sunday

derrière

behind	(place)	**derrière la maison**
		behind the house

dès

from	(time)	**dès six heures**
		from six o'clock onwards
		dès 1934
		as far back as 1934
		dès le début
		from the beginning
		dès maintenant
		from now on
	(place)	**dès Edimbourg**
		from (the moment of leaving) Edinburgh

devant

before/in front of	(place)	**devant l'école**
		in front of the school

en

in	(place)	**être en ville** to be in town **en Angleterre** in England
	(colour)	**un mur peint en jaune** a wall painted yellow
	(material)	**une montre en or** a gold watch
	(dates etc)	**en quelle année ?** in what year? **en 1986** in 1986 **en été, en juillet** in the summer, in July
	(dress)	**en bikini** in a bikini
	(language)	**en chinois** in Chinese
	(time)	**j'ai fait mes devoirs en 20 minutes** I did my homework in 20 minutes
by	(means)	**en auto/en avion** by car/by plane
like, as		**il s'est habillé en femme** he dressed as a woman
on	(idiom)	**en vacances** on holiday **en moyenne** on average
	(+ present participle)	**en faisant** on/while/by doing

Note: **en** *is not used with the definite article except in certain*
expressions: **en l'an 2000** *(in the year 2000),* **en l'honneur de** *(in*
honour of) and **en la présence de** *(in the presence of).*

en tant que

as/in (my) capacity as	**en tant que professeur** as a teacher

entre

among		**être entre amis** to be among friends
between	(place)	**entre Londres et Douvres** between London and Dover
	(time)	**entre 6 et 10 heures** between 6 and 10
	(idiom)	**entre toi et moi** between you and me
in	(punctuation)	**entre guillemets** in inverted commas **entre parenthèses** in brackets

d'entre

of/from among	**certains d'entre eux** some of them

envers

to/towards	**être bien disposé envers quelqu'un** to be well-disposed towards someone

hors de

out of	**hors de danger** out of danger

jusque

up to/as far as	(place)	**jusqu'à la frontière espagnole** as far as the Spanish border
	(time)	**jusqu'ici/jusque-là** up to now/up till then
till		**jusqu'à demain** till tomorrow

malgré

| in spite of | | **malgré la chaleur**
in spite of the heat |

par

by	(agent)	**la lettre a été envoyée par mon ami** the letter was sent by my friend
	(means of transport)	**par le train** by train
	(distributive)	**trois fois par semaine** three times a week
by		**deux par deux** two by two
	(place)	**par ici/là** this/that way
in/on	(weather)	**par un temps pareil** in such weather **par un beau jour d'hiver** on a beautiful winter's day
out of	(place)	**regarder par la fenêtre** to look out of the window **jeter du pain par la fenêtre** to throw bread out of the window
to/on		**tomber par terre** to fall to the ground **étendu par terre** lying on the ground
	(+ infinitive)	**commencer/finir par faire** to begin/end by doing

parmi

| among | | **parmi ses ennemis**
among his enemies |

pendant

for	(time)	**il l'avait fait pendant 5 années** he had done it for 5 years
during		**pendant l'été** during the summer

pour

for		**ce livre est pour vous** this book is for you **mourir pour la patrie** to die for one's country
	(purpose)	**c'est pour cela que je suis venu** that's why I have come
	(emphatic)	**pour moi, je crois que** personally, I think that
	(time)	**j'en ai pour une heure** it'll take me an hour **je serai là pour 2 semaines** I'll be here for 2 weeks
	(*pour* stresses intention and future time: see **depuis** and **pendant**, p 202 and above)	
	(idiom)	**c'est bon pour la santé** it's good for your health
to	(+ infinitive)	**il était trop paresseux pour réussir aux examens** he was too lazy to pass the exams

près de

near	(place)	**près du marché** near the market
nearly	(time)	**il est près de minuit** it's nearly midnight
	(quantity)	**près de cinquante** nearly fifty

quant à

as for	**quant à moi** as for me

sans

without	(+ noun)	**sans espoir** without hope
	(+ pronoun)	**je n'irai pas sans vous** I'll not go without you
	(+ infinitive)	**sans parler** without speaking **sans s'arrêter** without stopping

sauf

except for	**ils sont tous partis, sauf John** everyone left except John
barring	**sauf accidents/sauf imprévu** barring accidents/the unexpected

selon

according to	**selon le président** according to the President **selon moi** in my opinion

sous

under	(physical)	**sous la table** under the table
	(historical)	**sous Elisabeth II** under Elizabeth II
in	(weather)	**sous la pluie** in the rain
	(idiom)	**sous peu** shortly/before long **sous la main** to hand **sous tous les rapports** in all respects **sous mes yeux** before my eyes

sur

on/upon	(place)	**le bol est sur la table** the bowl is on the table
off		**prendre sur le rayon** to take off the shelf
out of	(proportion)	**neuf sur dix** nine out of ten **une semaine sur trois** one week in three
over	(place)	**le pont sur la Loire** the bridge over the Loire
about	(idiom)	**une enquête sur ...** an enquiry about ...
at		**sur ces paroles** at these words **sur ce, il est sorti** at this /whereupon he went out
by		**quatre mètres sur cinq** four metres by five
in		**sur un ton amer** in a bitter tone (of voice)

over		**l'emporter sur quelqu'un** to prevail over someone

vers

towards	(place)	**vers le nord** towards the north
	(time)	**vers la fin du match** towards the end of the match
about	(time)	**vers 10 heures** about 10 o'clock

voici/voilà

here	(is)	**le voici qui vient** here he comes
there	(is)	**voilà où il demeure** that is where he lives

9. CONJUNCTIONS

Conjunctions are words or expressions which link words, phrases or clauses. They fall into two categories:

    A. coordinating
    B. subordinating

A.   COORDINATING CONJUNCTIONS

1. Definition

These link two similar words or groups of words (eg nouns, pronouns, adjectives, adverbs, prepositions, phrases or clauses). The principal coordinating conjunctions (or adverbs used as conjunctions) are:

et and	**mais** but	**ou** or
ou bien or (else)	**soit** either	**ni** neither
alors then	**aussi** therefore	**donc** then, therefore
puis then (*next*)	**car** for (*because*)	**or** now
cependant however	**néanmoins** nevertheless	**pourtant** yet, however
toutefois however		

il est malade, mais il ne veut pas aller au lit
he's ill but he won't go to bed

il faisait beau, alors il est allé se promener
it was fine so he went for a walk

2. Repetition

a) Some coordinating conjunctions are repeated:

soit ... soit   either ... or

prenez soit l'un soit l'autre
take one or the other

ni ... ni   neither ... nor

le vieillard n'avait ni amis ni argent
the old man had neither friends nor money

b) **et** and **ou** can be repeated in texts of a literary nature:

et ... et   both ... and
ou ... ou   whether ... or

3. aussi

aussi means 'therefore' only when placed before the verb. The subject pronoun is placed after the verb (see p 228).

il pleuvait, aussi Pascal n'est-il pas sorti
it was raining, so Pascal didn't go out

When **aussi** follows the verb it means 'also':

j'ai aussi mis mon imperméable
I also put my raincoat on

B. SUBORDINATING CONJUNCTIONS

These join a subordinate clause to another clause, usually a main clause. The principal subordinating conjunctions are:

comme	as	**parce que**	because
puisque	since	**ainsi que**	(just) as
à mesure que	as	**tant que**	as long as
avant que	before	**après que**	after
jusqu'à ce que	until	**depuis que**	since
pendant que	while	**tandis que**	whereas
si	if	**à moins que**	unless
pourvu que	provided that	**quoique**	although
bien que	although	**quand**	when
lorsque	when	**dès que**	as soon as
aussitôt que	as soon as	**pour que**	in order that
afin que	so that	**de sorte que**	so that
de façon que	so that	**de peur que (+ ne)**	for fear that, lest

Note: some subordinating conjunctions require the subjunctive (see p 128-9).

C. QUE

que can be coordinating or subordinating:

1. coordinating, in comparisons (see p 44-6 and 54-5)

> **il est plus fort que moi**
> he is stronger than I

2. subordinating

a) *meaning 'that'*:

> **elle dit qu'elle l'a vu**　　**je pense que tu as raison**
> she says she has seen him　　I think you're right

> **il faut que tu viennes**
> you'll have to come

b) *replacing another conjunction*:

When a conjunction introduces more than one verb, **que** usually replaces the second (and subsequent) subordinating conjunctions to avoid repetition:

> **comme il était tard et que j'étais fatigué, je suis rentré**
> as it was late and I was tired, I went home

Note: the mood after **que** is the same as that taken by the conjunction it replaces, except in the case of **si** in which **que** requires the subjunctive:

> **s'il fait beau et que tu sois libre, nous irons à la piscine**
> if it's fine and you are free, we'll go to the swimming pool

10. NUMBERS AND QUANTITY

A. CARDINAL NUMBERS

0	zéro	40	quarante
1	un (une)	50	cinquante
2	deux	60	soixante
3	trois	70	soixante-dix
4	quatre	71	soixante et onze
5	cinq	72	soixante-douze
6	six	80	quatre-vingt(s)
7	sept	90	quatre-vingt-dix
8	huit	99	quatre-vingt-dix-neuf
9	neuf		
10	dix	100	cent
11	onze	101	cent un(e)
12	douze	102	cent deux
13	treize	121	cent vingt et un(e)
14	quatorze	122	cent vingt-deux
15	quinze	200	deux cents
16	seize	201	deux cent un(e)
17	dix-sept	1000	mille
18	dix-huit	1988	mille neuf cent quatre-vingt-huit
19	dix-neuf		
20	vingt		
30	trente	2000	deux mille
		10,000	dix mille
		1,000,000	un million

Note:

a) **un** is the only cardinal number which agrees with the noun in gender:

un kilo	**une pomme**
a kilo	an apple

b) hyphens are used in compound numbers between 17 and 99 except where **et** is used (this also applies to compound numbers after 100: **cent vingt-trois** 123).

c) **cent** and **mille** are not preceded by **un** as in English (one hundred).

d) **vingt** and **cent** multiplied by a number take an s when they are not followed by another number.

e) **mille** is invariable.

B. ORDINAL NUMBERS

		abbreviation
1st	**premier/première**	**1er/1ère**
2nd	**deuxième/second**	**2e**
3rd	**troisième**	**3e**
4th	**quatrième**	**4e**
5th	**cinquième**	**5e**
6th	**sixième**	**6e**
7th	**septième**	**7e**
8th	**huitième**	**8e**
9th	**neuvième**	**9e**
10th	**dixième**	**10e**
11th	**onzième**	**11e**
12th	**douzième**	**12e**
13th	**treizième**	**13e**
14th	**quatorzième**	**14e**
15th	**quinzième**	**15e**
16th	**seizième**	**16e**
17th	**dix-septième**	**17e**
18th	**dix-huitième**	**18e**
19th	**dix-neuvième**	**19e**
20th	**vingtième**	**20e**
21st	**vingt et unième**	**21e**
22nd	**vingt-deuxième**	**22e**
30th	**trentième**	**30e**
100th	**centième**	**100e**
101st	**cent unième**	**101e**
200th	**deux centième**	**200e**
1000th	**millième**	**1000e**
10,000th	**dix millième**	**10 000e**

Note:

a) ordinal numbers are formed by adding **-ième** to cardinal numbers, except for **premier** and **second**; **cinq**, **neuf** and numbers ending in **e** undergo slight changes: **cinquième**, **neuvième**, **onzième**, **douzième** etc.

b) ordinal numbers agree with the noun in gender and number:

    le premier ministre   **la première fleur du**
    the Prime Minister   **printemps**
                         the first flower of spring

c) there is no elision with **huitième** and **onzième**:

    le huitième jour   **du onzième candidat**
    the eighth day   of the eleventh candidate

d) cardinal numbers are used for monarchs, except for 'first':

    Charles deux   **Charles premier**
    Charles II   Charles I

C.   FRACTIONS AND PROPORTIONS

1.   Fractions

Fractions are expressed as in English: cardinal followed by ordinal:

deux cinquièmes
two fifths

But: ¼   **un quart**   ½   **un demi, une demie; la**
                                        moitié

        ⅓   **un tiers**   ¾   **trois quarts**

2.   Decimals

The English decimal point is conveyed by a comma in French:

un virgule huit (1,8)
one point eight (1.8)

3.   Approximate numbers

une huitaine   **une dizaine**
about eight   about ten

une trentaine   **une centaine**
some thirty   about a hundred

But: **un millier**
        about a thousand

Note: **de** is used when the approximate number is followed by a noun:

une vingtaine d'enfants
about twenty children

4.   Arithmetic

Addition:	**deux plus quatre**	2+4
Subtraction	**cinq moins deux**	5−2
Multiplication	**trois fois cinq**	3×5
Division	**six divisé par deux**	6÷2
Square	**deux au carré**	2^2

D.   MEASUREMENTS AND PRICES

1. Measurements

a) *Dimensions*

> **la salle de classe est longue de 12 mètres**
> **la salle de classe a/fait 12 mètres de longueur/de long**
> the classroom is 12 metres long

Similarly:

> **profond(e)/de profondeur/de profond**   deep
> **épais(se)/d'épaisseur**   thick
> **haut(e)/de hauteur/de haut**   high
>
> **ma chambre fait quatre mètres sur trois**
> my bedroom is about 4 metres by three

b) *Distance*

> **à quelle distance sommes-nous du lycée ?**
> how far are we from the secondary school!?
>
> **nous sommes à deux kilomètres du lycée**
> we are 2 kilometres from the secondary school
>
> **combien y a-t-il d'ici à Blois ?**
> how far is it to Blois?

2. Price

> **ce chandail m'a coûté 110 francs**
> this sweater cost me 110 francs
>
> **j'ai payé ce chandail 110 francs**
> I paid 110 francs for this sweater
>
> **des pommes à 10 francs le kilo**
> apples at 10 francs a kilo
>
> **du vin blanc à 12 francs la bouteille**
> white wine at 12 francs a bottle
>
> **cela fait/revient à 42 francs**
> that comes to 42 francs
>
> **ils coûtent 25 francs pièce**
> they cost 25 francs each

E. EXPRESSIONS OF QUANTITY

Quantity may be expressed by an adverb of quantity (eg 'a lot', 'too much') or by a noun which names the actual quantity involved (eg 'a bottle', 'a dozen').

1. Expression of quantity + 'de' + noun

Before a noun, adverbs and other expressions of quantity are followed by de (d' before a vowel or a silent h) and never by du, de la or des, except for bien des and la plupart du/des:

assez de enough	**autant de** as much/many
beaucoup de a lot of, much, many	**combien de** how much/many
moins de less, fewer	**plus de** more
peu de little, few	**un peu de** a little
tant de so much/many	**tellement de** so much/many
trop de too much/many	
bien du/de la/des many, a lot of	**la plupart du/de la/des** most

il y a assez de fromage ? is there enough cheese?	**j'ai beaucoup d'amis** I've got a lot of friends
je n'ai pas beaucoup de temps I haven't got much time	**il y a combien de pièces ?** how many rooms are there?
tu as combien d'argent ? how much money have you got?	**mange plus de légumes !** eat more vegetables!
il y avait peu de choix there was little choice	**peu de gens le savent** not many people know that

tu veux un peu de pain ?
would you like a little bread?

il y a tant d'années
so many years ago

j'ai trop de travail
I've got too much work

il y a trop de voitures
there are too many cars

bien des gens
a good many people

la plupart des Français
most French people

2. Noun expressing quantity + 'de' + noun

une boîte de
a box/tin/jar of

une bouteille de
a bottle of

une bouchée de
a mouthful of (*food*)

une cuillerée de
a spoonful of

une douzaine de
a dozen

une gorgée de
a mouthful of (*drink*)

un kilo de
a kilo of

un litre de
a litre of

une livre de
a pound of

un morceau de
a piece of

un paquet de
a packet of

une paire de
a pair of

une part de
a share/helping of

une tasse de
a cup of

une tranche de
a slice of

un verre de
a glass of

je voudrais une boîte de thon et un litre de lait
I'd like a tin of tuna fish and a litre of milk

il a mangé une douzaine d'œufs et six morceaux de poulet
he ate a dozen eggs and six pieces of chicken

3. Expressions of quantity used without a noun

When an expression of quantity is not followed by a noun, **de** is replaced by the pronoun **en** (see p 76):

il y avait beaucoup de neige ; il y en avait beaucoup
there was a lot of snow; there was a lot (of it)

elle a mangé trop de chocolats ; elle en a trop mangé
she's eaten too many chocolates; she's eaten too many (of them)

11. EXPRESSIONS OF TIME

A. THE TIME

quelle heure est-il ?   what time is it?

a) *full hours*

    il est midi/minuit   **il est une heure**
    it is 12 noon (midday)/   it is 1 o'clock
    midnight

b) *half-hours*

    il est minuit et demi(e)   **il est midi et demi(e)**
    it is 12.30 a.m.   it is 12.30 p.m.

    il est une heure et demie
    it is 1.30

c) *quarter-hours*

    il est deux heures un/   **il est deux heures moins**
    et quart   **le/un quart**
    it is a quarter past two   it is a quarter to two

d) *minutes*

    il est quatre heures   **il est cinq heures moins**
    vingt-trois   **vingt**
    it's 23 minutes past 4   it is 20 to 5

Note: **minutes** is usually omitted; **heures** is never omitted.

e) *a.m. and p.m.*

    du matin   **de l'après-midi/du soir**
    a.m.   p.m.

    il est sept heures dix du soir   **il est sept heures moins dix**
    it is 7.10 p.m.   **du matin**
                                          it is 6.50 a.m.

The 24 hour clock is commonly used:

dix heures trente
10.30 a.m.

quatorze heures trente-cinq
2.35 p.m.

dix-neuf heures dix
7.10 p.m.

Note: times are often abbreviated as follows:

dix-neuf heures dix   **19h10**

B.   THE DATE

1.   Names of months, days and seasons

a) *Months (les mois)*

janvier	January
février	February
mars	March
avril	April
mai	May
juin	June
juillet	July
août	August
septembre	September
octobre	October
novembre	November
décembre	December

b) *Days of the week (les jours de la semaine)*

lundi	Monday
mardi	Tuesday
mercredi	Wednesday
jeudi	Thursday
vendredi	Friday
samedi	Saturday
dimanche	Sunday

c) *Seasons (les saisons)*

le printemps (spring)	**l'été** (summer)
l'automne (autumn)	**l'hiver** (winter)

For prepositions used with the seasons see p 17.

Note: in French the months and days are masculine and do not have a capital letter, unless they begin a sentence.

2.   Dates

a) cardinals (eg **deux**, **trois**) are used for the dates of the month except the first:

le quatorze juillet	**le deux novembre**
the fourteenth of July	the second of November

But: **le premier février**
the first of February

The definite article is used as in English; French does not use
prepositions ('on' and 'of' in English):

je vous ai écrit le trois mars
I wrote to you on the third of March

b) **mil** (a thousand) may be used instead of **mille** in dates from 1001
onwards:

mil neuf cent quatre-vingt sept
nineteen hundred and eighty-seven

3. Année, journée, matinée, soirée

Année, journée, matinée, soirée (the feminine forms of **an**, **jour**,
matin and **soir**) are usually found in the following cases:

a) *when duration is implied* (eg the whole day):

pendant une année	for a (whole) year
toute la journée	all day long
dans la matinée	in the (course of the) morning
passer une soirée	to spend an evening
l'année scolaire/ universitaire	the school/academic year

b) *with an ordinal number* (eg *première*) *or an indefinite expression:*

la deuxième année	the second year
dans sa vingtième année	in his twentieth year
plusieurs/quelques années	several/a few years
bien des/de nombreuses années	many years
environ une année	about a year

c) *with an adjective:*

de bonnes/mauvaises années	good/bad years

C. IDIOMATIC EXPRESSIONS

à cinq heures	at 5 o'clock
à onze heures environ	about 11 o'clock
vers minuit	about midnight
vers (les) dix heures	about 10 o'clock
il est six heures passées	it is past 6 o'clock
à quatre heures précises/pile	at exactly 4 o'clock
il est neuf heures sonnées	it has struck nine
sur le coup de trois heures	on the stroke of three
à partir de neuf heures	from 9 o'clock onwards
peu avant sept heures	shortly before seven
peu après sept heures	shortly after seven
tôt ou tard	sooner or later
au plus tôt	at the earliest
au plus tard	at the latest
il est tard	it is late
il est en retard	he is late
il se lève tard	he gets up late
il est arrivé en retard	he arrived late
le train a vingt minutes de retard	the train is twenty minutes late
ma montre retarde de six minutes	my watch is six minutes slow
ma montre avance de six minutes	my watch is six minutes fast
ce soir	tonight
demain soir	tomorrow night
hier soir	yesterday evening, last night
demain matin	tomorrow morning
demain en huit	tomorrow week
le lendemain	the next day
le lendemain matin	the next morning
hier matin	yesterday morning
la semaine dernière	last week
la semaine prochaine	next week
lundi	on Monday
le lundi	on Mondays
il y a trois semaines	three weeks ago
une demi-heure	a half-hour, half an hour

un quart d'heure	a quarter of an hour
trois quarts d'heure	three quarters of an hour
passer son temps (à faire)	to spend one's time (doing)
perdre son temps	to waste one's time
de temps en temps	from time to time
tous les samedis	every Saturday
tous les samedis soirs	every Saturday evening/night
le combien sommes-nous aujourd'hui ?	what's the date today?
nous sommes/c'est le trois avril	it is the third of April
le vendredi treize juillet	Friday the thirteenth of July
en février/au mois de février	in February/in the month of February
en 1970	in 1970
dans les années soixante	in the sixties
au dix-septième siècle	in the seventeenth century
au XVIIe	in the 17th C
le jour de l'An	New Year's Day
avoir treize ans	to be thirteen years old
être âgé de quatorze ans	to be fourteen years old
elle fête ses vingt ans	she's celebrating her twentieth birthday
un plan quinquennal	a five-year plan
une année bissextile	a leap year
une année civile	a calendar year
une année-lumière	a light year

12. THE SENTENCE

A. WORD ORDER

Word order is usually the same in French as in English, except in the following cases:

1. Adjectives

Many French adjectives follow the noun (see p 41-3):

de l'argent *italien*	j'ai les yeux *bleus*
(some) *Italian* money	I've got *blue* eyes

2. Adverbs

In simple tenses, adverbs usually follow the verb (see p 53):

j'y vais *rarement*	il fera *bientôt* nuit
I *seldom* go there	it will *soon* be dark

3. Object pronouns

Object pronouns usually come before the verb (see p 72):

je *t'*attendrai	il *la* lui a vendue
I'll wait *for you*	he sold *it* to him

4. Noun phrases

Noun phrases are formed differently in French (see p 247):

une chemise en coton	le père de mon copain
a cotton shirt	my friend's father

5. Exclamations

The word order is not affected after **que** or **comme** (unlike after 'how' in English):

que tu es bête !	qu'il fait froid !
you are silly!	it's so cold!
(how silly you are!)	
comme il chante mal !	comme c'est beau !
he sings so badly!	that's so beautiful!

6. DONT

dont must be followed by the subject of the clause it introduces; compare:

> **l'agence d'emploi dont j'ai perdu la lettre**
> the employment agency whose letter I lost

> **l'agence d'emploi dont la lettre est arrivée hier**
> the employment agency whose letter arrived yesterday

7. Inversion

In certain cases, the subject of a French clause is placed after the verb. Word order is effectively that of an interrogative sentence (see p 234). This occurs:

a) *after the following, but only when they start a clause:*

à peine	**aussi**	**peut-être**
hardly	therefore	maybe, perhaps

> **à peine Alain était-il sorti qu'il a commencé à pleuvoir**
> Alain had hardly gone out when it started raining

> **il y avait une grève du métro, aussi a-t-il pris un taxi**
> there was an underground strike, so he took a taxi

> **peut-être vont-ils téléphoner plus tard**
> maybe they'll phone later

But: **Alain était à peine sorti qu'il a commencé à pleuvoir**

> **ils vont peut-être téléphoner plus tard**

b) *when a verb of saying follows direct speech:*

> **"si tu veux", a répondu Marie**
> 'if you want', Marie replied

> **"attention !" a-t-elle crié**
> 'watch out!', she shouted

> **"j'espère que non", dit-il**
> 'I hope not', he said

> **"répondez !" ordonna-t-il**
> 'answer!', he ordered

B. NEGATIVE EXPRESSIONS

1. Main negative words

a)

ne ... pas	not
ne ... point	not (*literary*)
ne ... plus	no more/longer, not ... any more
ne ... jamais	never
ne ... rien	nothing, not ... anything
ne ... guère	hardly

b)

ne ... personne	nobody, no one, not ... anyone
ne ... que	only
ne ... ni	neither ... nor
(ni ... ni)	
ne ... aucun(e)	no, not any, none
ne ... nul(le)	no
ne ... nulle part	nowhere, not ... anywhere

Note:

i) **ne** becomes **n'** before a vowel or a silent **h**

ii) **aucun** and **nul**, like other adjectives and pronouns, agree with the word they refer to; they are only used in the singular.

2. Position of negative expressions

a) *with simple tenses and with the imperative*

negative words enclose the verb: **ne** comes before the verb, and the second part of the negative expression comes after the verb:

je ne la connais pas I don't know her	**n'insistez pas !** don't insist!
je n'ai plus d'argent I haven't any money left	**tu ne le sauras jamais** you'll never know
ne dis rien don't say anything	**il n'y a personne** no one's here
je n'avais que dix francs I only had ten francs	**il n'est nulle part** it isn't anywhere
tu n'as aucun sens de l'humour you have no sense of humour	**ce n'est ni noir ni bleu** it's neither black nor blue

b) *with compound tenses*

with **ne ... pas** and the other expressions in list **1a**, the word order is: **ne** + auxiliary + **pas** + past participle:

il n'est pas revenu
he didn't come back

je n'ai plus essayé
I didn't try any more

je n'avais jamais vu Paris
I had never seen Paris

on n'a rien fait
we haven't done anything

with **ne ... personne** and the other expressions in list **1b**, the word order is: **ne** + auxiliary + past participle + **personne/que/ni** etc:

il ne l'a dit à personne
he didn't tell anyone

tu n'en as acheté qu'un ?
did you only buy one?

je n'en ai aimé aucun
I didn't like any of them

il n'est allé nulle part
he hasn't gone anywhere

c) *with the infinitive*

i) **ne ... pas** and the other expressions in list **1a** are placed together before the verb:

je préfère ne pas y aller
I'd rather not go

essaye de ne rien perdre
try not to lose anything

ii) **ne ... personne** and the other expressions in list **1b** enclose the infinitive:

il a été surpris de ne voir personne
he was surprised not to see anybody

j'ai décidé de n'en acheter aucun
I decided not to buy any of them

d) *at the beginning of a sentence*

when **personne**, **rien**, **aucun** and **ni ... ni** begin a sentence, they are followed by **ne**:

personne ne le sait
nobody knows

rien n'a changé
nothing has changed

**ni Paul ni Simone
ne sont venus**
neither Paul nor Simone
came

aucun secours n'est arrivé
no help arrived

3. Combination of negative expressions

Negative expressions can be combined:

ne ... plus jamais
ne ... plus rien
ne ... plus personne
ne ... plus ni ... ni
ne ... plus que

ne ... jamais rien
ne ... jamais personne
ne ... jamais ni ... ni
ne ... jamais que

on ne l'a plus jamais revu
we never saw him again

il n'y a plus rien
there isn't anything left

plus personne ne viendra
no one will come any more

tu ne dis jamais rien
you never say anything

**je ne bois jamais que
de l'eau**
I only ever drink water

je ne vois jamais personne
I never see anybody

4. Negative expressions without a verb

a) PAS

pas (not) is the most common of all negatives; it is frequently used
without a verb:

**tu l'aimes ? — pas
beaucoup**
do you like it? — not much

ah non, pas lui !
oh no, not him!

non merci, pas pour moi
no thanks, not for me

un roman pas très long
not a very long novel

lui, il viendra, mais pas moi
he will come, but I won't

j'aime ça ; pas toi ?
I like that; don't you?

b) NE

ne is not used when there is no verb:

qui a crié ? — personne
who shouted? — nobody

jamais de la vie !
not on your life!

rien ! je ne veux rien !
nothing! I want nothing!

rien du tout
nothing at all

c) *NON*

non (no) is always used without a verb:

> **tu aimes la natation ? — non, pas du tout**
> do you like swimming? — no, not at all

> **tu viens, oui ou non ?**   **je crois que non**
> are you coming, yes or no?   I don't think so

Note: **non plus** = 'neither':

> **je ne le crois pas — moi non plus**
> I don't believe him — neither do I

> **je n'ai rien mangé — nous non plus**
> I haven't eaten anything — neither have we

C. DIRECT AND INDIRECT QUESTIONS

1. Direct questions

There are three ways of forming direct questions in French:

    a) subject + verb (+ question word)
    b) (question word) + **est-ce que** + subject + verb
    c) (question word) + verb + subject = inversion

a) *subject + verb (+ question word)*

The word order remains the same as in statements (subject + verb) but the intonation changes: the voice is raised at the end of the sentence. This is by far the most common question form in conversational French:

tu l'as acheté où ?
where did you buy it?

je peux téléphoner d'ici ?
can I phone from here?

vous prendrez quel train ?
which train will you take?

tu lui fais confiance ?
do you trust him?

c'était comment ?
what was it like?

la gare est près d'ici ?
is the station near here?

le train part à quelle heure ?
what time does the train leave?

cette robe me va ?
does this dress suit me?

b) *(question word) + est-ce que + subject + verb*

This question form is also very common in conversation:

qu'est-ce que tu as ?
what's the matter with you?

est-ce qu'il est là ?
is he in?

est-ce que ton ami s'est amusé ?
did your friend have a good time?

où est-ce que vous avez mal ?
where does it hurt?

c) *inversion*

This question form is the most formal of the three, and the least commonly used in conversation.

i) if the subject is a pronoun, word order is as follows:

(question word) + verb + hyphen + subject

où allez-vous ?	**voulez-vous commander ?**
where are you going?	do you wish to order?
quand est-il arrivé ?	**avez-vous bien dormi ?**
when did he arrive?	did you sleep well?

ii) if the subject is a noun, a pronoun referring to the noun is inserted after the verb, and linked to it with a hyphen:

(question word) + noun subject + verb + hyphen + pronoun

où ton père travaillait-il ?	**Nicole en veut-elle ?**
where did your father work?	does Nicole want any?

iii) **-t-** is inserted before **il** and **elle** when the verb ends in a vowel:

comment va-t-il voyager ?	**aime-t-elle le café ?**
how will he travel?	does she like coffee?
pourquoi a-t-il refusé ?	**Marie viendra-t-elle ?**
why did he refuse?	will Marie be coming?

Note: when a question word is used, modern French will often just invert verb and noun subject, without adding a pronoun; no hyphen is then necessary:

où travaille ton père ?
where does your father work?

2. Indirect questions

a) *Definition*

Indirect questions follow a verb and are introduced by an interrogative (question) word, eg:

ask him when he will arrive   I don't know why he did it

b) *Word order*

i) The word order is usually the same as in statements: question word + subject + verb:

je ne sais pas s'il voudra	**dis-moi où tu l'as mis**
I don't know if he'll want to	tell me where you put it

il n'a pas dit quand il appellerait
he didn't say when he would phone

ii) If the subject is a noun, verb and subject are sometimes inverted:

demande-leur où est le camping
ask them where the campsite is

But: **je ne comprends pas comment l'accident s'est produit**
I don't understand how the accident happened

il ne savait pas pourquoi les magasins étaient fermés
he didn't know why the shops were closed

3. Translation of English question tags

a) Examples of question tags are: isn't it? aren't you? doesn't he? won't they? haven't you? is it? did you? etc.

b) French doesn't use question tags as often as English. Some of them can however be translated in the following ways:

i) **n'est-ce pas ?**

n'est-ce pas ? is used at the end of a sentence when confirmation of a statement is expected:

c'était très intéressant, n'est-ce pas ?
it was very interesting, wasn't it?

tu voudrais trouver un emploi stable, n'est-ce pas ?
you would like to find a secure job, wouldn't you?

vous n'arriverez pas trop tard, n'est-ce pas ?
you won't be arriving too late, will you?

ii) **hein ?** and **non ?**

In conversation **hein ?** and **non ?** are often used after affirmative statements instead of **n'est-ce pas** :

il fait beau, hein ?	**il est amusant, non ?**
it's nice weather, isn't it?	he's funny, isn't he?

D. ANSWERS ('YES' AND 'NO')

1. OUI, SI and NON

a) **oui** and **si** mean 'yes' and are equivalent to longer positive answers such as: 'yes, it is', 'yes, I will', 'yes, he has' etc:

> **tu m'écriras ? — oui, bien sûr !**
> will you write to me? — (yes) of course I will

b) **non** means 'no' and is equivalent to longer negative answers such as: 'no, it isn't', 'no, I didn't' etc:

> **c'était bien ? — non, on s'est ennuyé(s)**
> was it good? — no, it wasn't; we were bored

2. OUI or SI?

oui and **si** both mean 'yes', but **oui** is used to answer an affirmative question, and **si** to contradict a negative question:

> **cette place est libre ? — oui**
> is this seat free? — yes (it is)

> **tu n'aimes pas lire ? — si, bien sûr !**
> don't you like reading? — yes, of course (I do)

13. TRANSLATION PROBLEMS

A. GENERAL TRANSLATION PROBLEMS

1. French words not translated in English

Some French words are not translated in English, particularly:

a) *Articles*

Definite and indefinite articles are not always translated (see p 16-20):

> **dans** *la* **société moderne,** *les* **prix sont élevés**
> in modern society, prices are high

> **ah non ! encore** *du* **riz ! je déteste** *le* **riz !**
> oh no! rice again! I hate rice!

b) *que*

que meaning 'that' as a conjunction (see p 213) or 'that'/'which'/'whom' as a relative pronoun (see p 86) cannot be omitted in French:

> **j'espère** *que* **tu vas mieux**
> I hope you're better

> **celui** *que* **j'ai vu**
> the one I saw

> **elle pense** *que* **c'est vrai**
> she thinks it's true

> **c'est un pays** *que* **j'aime**
> it's a country I like

c) *Prepositions*

Some French verbs are followed by a preposition (+ indirect object) when their English equivalent takes a direct object (without preposition) (see p 193-4):

> **elle a téléphoné** *au* **médecin**
> she phoned the doctor

> **tu l'as dit** *à* **ton père ?**
> did you tell your father?

d) *le*

When **le** (it) is used in an impersonal sense (see p 72), it is not translated:

oui, je *le* sais	**dis-*le*-lui**
yes, I know	tell him

2. English words not translated in French

Some English words are not translated in French, for example:

a) *Prepositions*

i) with verbs which take an indirect object in English, but a direct object in French (see p 192):

tu l'as payé combien ?	**écoutez cette chanson**
how much did you pay *for* it?	listen *to* this song

ii) in certain expressions (see p 225-6):

je viendrai te voir lundi soir
I'll come and see you *on* Monday night

b) *'can'*

'can' + verb of hearing or seeing (see p 154):

je ne vois rien !	**tu entends la musique ?**
I can't see anything	can you hear the music?

3. Other differences

a) *English phrasal verbs*

Phrasal verbs are verbs which, when followed by a preposition, take on a different meaning, eg 'to give up', 'to walk out'. They do not exist in French and are translated by simple verbs or by expressions:

to give up	to run away	to run across
abandonner	**s'enfuir**	**traverser en courant**

b) *English possessive adjectives*

English possessive adjectives (my, your etc) are translated by the French definite article (**le/la/les**) when parts of the body are mentioned (see p 82):

brush *your* teeth	he hurt *his* foot
brosse-toi *les* **dents**	**il s'est fait mal** *au* **pied**

c) *'from'*

'from' is translated by **à** with verbs of 'taking away' (see p 195):

he hid it *from* his parents	borrow some *from* your dad
il l'a caché *à* **ses parents**	**empruntes-en** *à* **ton père**

B.   SPECIFIC TRANSLATION PROBLEMS

1.   Words in -ing

The English verb form ending in **-ing** is translated in a number of ways in French:

a) *by the appropriate French tense* (see p 117):

he's speaking (present tense)	**il parle**
he was speaking (imperfect)	**il parlait**
he will be speaking (future)	**il parlera**
he has been speaking (perfect)	**il a parlé**
he had been speaking (pluperfect)	**il avait parlé**
he would be speaking (conditional)	**il parlerait**

b) *by a French present participle* (see p 145)

i) as an adjective:

un livre amusant   **c'est effrayant**
a funny book   it's frightening

ii) as a verb, with **en** (while/on/by doing something; see p 145-6):

"ça ne fait rien", dit-il en souriant
'it doesn't matter', he said smiling

j'ai vu mes copains en sortant du lycée
I saw my friends while (I was) coming out of school

But: **en** + present participle cannot be used when the two verbs have different subjects, eg:

I saw my brother coming out of school
j'ai vu mon frère sortir du lycée/qui sortait du lycée

c) *by a present infinitive* (see p 136-43):

i) after a preposition:

au lieu de rire   **avant de traverser**
instead of laughing   before crossing

ii) after verbs of perception:

je l'ai entendu appeler   **je l'ai vue entrer**
I heard him calling   I saw her going in

iii) after verbs of liking and disliking:

j'adore faire du camping
I love camping

tu aimes lire ?
do you like reading?

iv) after verbs followed by **à** or **de**:

tu passes tout ton temps à ne rien faire
you spend all your time doing nothing

il a commencé à neiger
it started snowing

continuez à travailler
go on working

tu as envie de sortir ?
do you feel like going out?

il doit finir de manger
he must finish eating

v) when an English verb in **-ing** is the subject of another verb:

attendre serait inutile
waiting would be pointless

écrire est une corvée !
writing is a real chore!

vi) when an English verb in **-ing** follows 'is' or 'was' etc:

mon passe-temps favori, c'est d'aller à la discothèque
my favourite pastime is going to the disco

d) *by a perfect infinitive* (see p 144)

i) after **après** (after):

j'ai pris une douche après avoir nettoyé ma chambre
I had a shower after cleaning my room

ii) after certain verbs:

regretter
to regret

remercier de
to thank for

se souvenir de
to remember

e) *by a noun*

particularly when referring to sports, activities, hobbies etc:

le ski
skiing

la natation
swimming

l'équitation
horse-riding

la voile
sailing

le patinage
skating

le canoë
canoeing

la lecture
reading

la planche à voile
wind-surfing

la cuisine
cooking

la boxe
boxing

la lutte
wrestling

la marche à pied
walking

2. IT IS (IT'S)

'it is' (it's) can be translated in three ways in French:

    a) **il/elle** + **être**
    b) **ce** + **être**
    c) **il** + **être**

a) *il or elle* (see p 71)

il or **elle** are used with the verb **être** to translate 'it is', 'it was' etc (+ adjective) when referring to a particular masculine or feminine noun (a thing, a place etc):

    merci de ta carte ; elle était très amusante
    thanks for your card; it was very funny

    regarde ce blouson ; il n'est vraiment pas cher
    look at that bomber jacket; it really isn't expensive

b) *ce* (see p 58-9)

ce (**c'** before a vowel) is used with the verb **être** to translate 'it is', 'it was' etc in two cases:

i) if **être** is followed by a word which is not an adjective on its own, ie by a noun, a pronoun, an expression of place etc:

c'était sa voix	**c'est une grande maison**
it was his voice	it's a big house
c'est moi ! c'est Claude !	**c'est le tien ?**
it's me! it's Claude!	is it yours?
c'est en France que tu vas ?	**c'est pour lundi**
is it France you're going to?	it's for Monday

ii) if **être** is followed by an adjective which refers to something previously mentioned, an idea, an event, a fact, but not to a specific noun:

    l'homme n'ira jamais sur Saturne ; ce n'est pas possible
    man will never go to Saturn; it's not possible

    j'ai passé mes vacances en Italie ; c'était formidable !
    I spent my holidays in Italy; it was great!

    oh, je m'excuse ! — ce n'est pas grave
    oh, I'm sorry! — it's all right

c) *il* (see p 113-6)

il is used to translate 'it is', 'it was' etc in three cases:

i) with **être** followed by an adjective + **de** or **que** (ie referring to something that follows, but not to a specific noun):

> **il est impossible de connaître l'avenir**
> it's impossible to know the future

> **il est évident que tu ne me crois pas**
> it's obvious you don't believe me

ii) to describe the weather (see p 113):

il y a du vent	**il faisait très froid**
it's windy	it was very cold

iii) with **être** to tell the time and in phrases relating to the time of day, or in such expressions as **il est temps de** (it's time to):

il est deux heures du matin	**ah bon ! il est tard !**
it's two a.m.	really! it's late!

> **il est temps de partir**
> it's time to go

Note: with other expressions of time, **c'est** is used:

c'est lundi ou mardi ?	**c'était l'été**
is it Monday or Tuesday?	it was summer

3. TO BE

Although 'to be' is usually translated by **être**, it can also be translated in the following ways:

a) *avoir*

i) **avoir** is used instead of **être** in many set expressions:

avoir faim/soif	to be hungry/thirsty
avoir chaud/froid	to be warm/cold
avoir peur/honte	to be afraid/ashamed
avoir tort/raison	to be right/wrong

ii) **avoir** is also used for age:

quel âge as-tu ?	**j'ai vingt-cinq ans**
how old are you?	I'm twenty five

b) *aller*

aller is used for describing health:

je vais mieux	**tout le monde va bien**
I am/feel better	everyone's fine

c) *faire*

faire is used in many expressions to describe the weather (see p 113):

il fait beau	**il fera chaud**
it's fine	it will be hot

Note: **il y a** can also be used to describe the weather, but only before **du/de la/des**:

il y a du vent/des nuages/de la tempête
it's windy/cloudy/stormy

d) *untranslated*

'to be' is not translated when it is the first part of an English continuous tense; instead, the appropriate tense is used in French (see p 117):

I'm having a bath	he was driving slowly
je prends un bain	**il conduisait lentement**

4. ANY

'any' can be translated in three different ways:

a) *du/de la/des* or *de* (see p 21-2)

the partitive article is used with a noun in negative and interrogative sentences:

il ne mange jamais de viande	**tu veux du pain ?**
he never eats any meat	do you want any bread?

b) *en* (see p 76)

en is used to translate 'any' without a noun in negative and interrogative sentences:

je n'en ai pas	**il en reste ?**
I haven't got any	is there any left?

c) *n'importe quel(le)s/quel(le)s or tout(e)/tou(te)s*

these are used to translate 'any' (and 'every') when they mean 'no matter which':

> **il pourrait arriver à n'importe quel moment**
> he could be arriving any time

> **prends n'importe quelle couleur, je les aime toutes**
> take any colour, I like them all

5. ANYONE, ANYTHING, ANYWHERE

Like 'any', these can be translated in different ways:

a) *in interrogative sentences:*

> **il y a quelqu'un ?** **tu l'as vu quelque part ?**
> is anyone in? did you see it anywhere?

> **il a dit quelque chose ?**
> did he say anything?

b) *in negative sentences:*

> **il n'y a personne** **je ne le vois nulle part**
> there isn't anyone I can't see it anywhere

> **je n'ai rien fait**
> I didn't do anything

c) *in the sense of 'any' (and 'every'), 'no matter which':*

> **n'importe qui peut le faire** **il croit n'importe quoi**
> anyone can do that he believes anything

> **j'irai n'importe où** **n'importe quand**
> I'll go anywhere anytime

6. YOU, YOUR, YOURS, YOURSELF

French has two separate sets of words to translate 'you', 'your', 'yours', 'yourself':

> a) **tu, te (t'), toi, ton/ta/tes, le tien** etc
> b) **vous, votre/vos, le vôtre** etc

For their respective meanings and uses, see p 70-72, 78, 81-3.

a) *tu etc*

tu, te, ton etc correspond to the **tu** form of the verb (second person singular) and are used when speaking to one person you know well (a friend, a relative) or to someone younger. They represent the familiar form of address:

tu viens au concert avec *ton* copain, Annie ? alors, je *t'*achète deux places ; une pour *toi* et une pour lui

are *you* coming to the concert with *your* boyfriend, Annie? well, then, I'll get *you* two seats: one for *you* and one for him

b) *vous etc*

vous, vos etc correspond to the **vous** form of the verb (second person plural) and are used:

i) when speaking to more than one person:

dépêchez-*vous*, les gars ! *vous* allez manquer le train
hurry up, boys! *you*'ll miss the train

ii) when speaking to one person you do not know well or to someone older. They represent the formal or polite form of address:

je regrette, Monsieur, mais *vous* ne pouvez pas garder *votre* chien avec *vous* dans ce restaurant

I'm sorry, sir, but *you* can't keep *your* dog with *you* in this restaurant

c) when speaking or writing to one person, you must not mix words from both sets, but decide whether you are being formal or familiar, and use the same form of address throughout:

Cher Michel,
Merci de ta lettre. Comment vas-*tu* ? ...
Dear Michel,
Thanks for *your* letter. How are *you*? ...

Monsieur,
Pourriez-*vous* me réserver une chambre dans *votre* hôtel pour le huit juin ?
Dear Sir,
Could *you* book a room for me in *your* hotel for the eighth of June?

vous etc and **tu** etc can only be used together when **vous** is plural (ie when it refers to more than one person):

> *tu* sais, Jean, *toi* et *ta* sœur, *vous vous* ressemblez
> *you* know, Jean, *you* and *your* sister look like *each other*

7. Noun phrases

A noun phrase is a combination of two nouns used together to name things or people. In English, the first of these nouns is used to describe the second one, eg 'a love story'. In French, however, the position of the two nouns is reversed, so that the describing noun comes second and is linked to the first one by the preposition **de** (or **d'**):

> **une histoire d'amour**
> a love story

un magasin de disques a record shop	**un acteur de cinéma** a film actor
un arrêt d'autobus a bus stop	**un film d'aventure** an adventure film
un coup de soleil sunstroke	**une boule de neige** a snowball
un roman de science-fiction a science fiction novel	**un match de football** a football game
le château d'Edimbourg Edinburgh castle	**un conte de fées** a fairy tale
un joueur de rugby a rugby player	**un employé de bureau** an office clerk

Note: when the describing noun refers to a material, the preposition **en** is often used instead of **de**:

un pull en laine a woollen jumper	**un pantalon en cuir** leather trousers
une bague en or a gold ring	**un sac en plastique** a plastic bag

8. Possession

In English, possession is often expressed by using a noun phrase and tagging **'s** at the end of the first word, eg:

>   my friend's cat

This is translated in French by: object + **de** + possessor:

>   **le chat de mon ami**

Note the use of the article **le/la/les**.

le fiancé de ma sœur	**les amis de Chantal**
my sister's fiancé	Chantal's friends

les événements de la semaine dernière
last week's events

When **'s** is used in the sense of 'someone's house' or 'shop' etc, it is translated by the preposition **chez**:

je téléphone de chez Paul	**chez le dentiste**
I'm telephoning from Paul's	at/to the dentist's

INDEX

HARRAP'S FRENCH STUDY AIDS

Also available in this series

FRENCH VOCABULARY

★ Ideal revision aid
★ Particularly suitable for exam revision
★ 6000 vocabulary items in 64 themes

142mm × 96mm/256pp/plastic cover
ISBN 0 245-54583-2
in USA 0-13-383290-2

FRENCH VERBS

★ Over 200 verbs fully conjugated
★ Index of 2400 common verbs
★ Notes on verb construction

142mm × 96mm/256pp/plastic cover
ISBN 0 245-54581-6
in USA 0-13-383308-9

MINI FRENCH DICTIONARY

★ For quick and easy reference
★ Clear layout
★ Handy format

142mm × 96mm/667pp/plastic cover
ISBN 0 245-54507-7
in USA 0-13-383142-6